Contents

"An extraordinarily valuable book for anyone seeking a stronger, more positive sense of self. Here you can learn not only to quiet the inner critic and embrace imperfection, but to build true self-compassion and a life of full engagement."

—**Matthew McKay, PhD**, coauthor of *Self-Esteem*

"*Embrace Your Greatness* is an easy-to-read and effective step-by-step guide to harboring greatness and improved self-esteem. Judith Belmont does an excellent job giving fifty practical exercises for everyone to be able to move toward a happier, more fulfilling life."

—**Susanne Babbel, PhD**, author of *Heal the Body, Heal the Mind*

"This book will be a very useful complement to a comprehensive self-esteem program, and an important addition to self-esteem literature."

—**Glenn R. Schiraldi, PhD**, retired professor for the University of Maryland School of Public Health, and author of *The Self-Esteem Workbook*, *The Resilience Workbook*, and *The Post-Traumatic Stress Disorder Sourcebook*

"Judith Belmont has written yet another book that hits the nail on the head. This book is a masterpiece full of specific strategies for all of us who ever struggle to improve and maintain healthy self-esteem (that's most of us). It addresses ten key areas that impact self-esteem and provides easy-to-use, proven strategies to help us feel good about ourselves and truly embrace our greatness. This book is perfect for anyone who needs help with self-worth, perfectionism, negative thoughts, preventing the past from interfering with the present, being mindful and present, self-care and kindness, assertiveness, relationships, and self-love. Psychotherapists will love this book and the fifty-plus strategies they can immediately use with their clients."

—**Debra Burdick, LCSW, BCN**, author of *Mindfulness Skills Workbook for Clinicians and Clients*, *Mindfulness for Teens with ADHD*, *Mindfulness for Kids with ADHD*, *ADHD Non-Medication Treatments and Skills*, and *Mindfulness for Kids Card Deck*

"*Embrace Your Greatness* has actionable tips presented in fifty straightforward, nonintimidating exercises to improve self-esteem. Judith's approachable tone engages readers in a way that encourages them to complete the exercises. The questions at the end of each section provide takeaways and additional reinforcement. We especially love number twelve: using a drop of food coloring in a glass of water to see how one negative thought can influence our perspective. This is a great resource for a quick pick-me-up, as well as long-term change."

—**Kelly and Michelle Skeen, PsyD**, coauthors of *Just As You Are*

"Judith Belmont's *Embrace Your Greatness* offers a comprehensive tutorial on building healthy self-esteem in an easy-to-read format and a compassionate voice. It presents ten facets of healthy self-esteem, and then helps the reader personalize them with step-by-step instructions for practicing each subset. It's a book you can pick up anytime and take a few healthy bites from without becoming overwhelmed."

—**Lisa M. Schab, LCSW**, psychotherapist in private practice, and author of *The Self-Esteem Workbook for Teens*, *Self-Esteem for Teens*, and *The Self-Esteem Habit for Teens*

50 WAYS to BUILD
UNSHAKABLE SELF-ESTEEM

JUDITH BELMONT, MS

New Harbinger Publications, Inc.

Publisher's Note

This publication is designed to provide accurate and authoritative information in regard to the subject matter covered. It is sold with the understanding that the publisher is not engaged in rendering psychological, financial, legal, or other professional services. If expert assistance or counseling is needed, the services of a competent professional should be sought.

Distributed in Canada by Raincoast Books

Copyright © 2019 by Judith Belmont
                    New Harbinger Publications, Inc.
                    5674 Shattuck Avenue
                    Oakland, CA 94609
                    www.newharbinger.com

Cover design by Amy Shoup

Acquired by Wendy Millstine and Jennye Garibaldi

Edited by Cindy Nixon

Library of Congress Cataloging-in-Publication Data on file

20   19   18

10   9   8   7   6   5   4   3   2   1   First Printing

Contents

Introduction

This book is about you!

I am happy to offer you a practical guide on how to embrace your greatness, in which you will learn ways to identify and overcome the mental blocks that prevent you from truly loving yourself. You will learn how to put an end to the self-critical beliefs and actions that keep you stuck, overwhelmed, and defeated. I wrote this book because, after more than forty years as a psychotherapist, I see low self-esteem as the number one culprit underlying almost all common life problems, leading to crippling self-doubt and self-sabotaging behaviors. Low self-esteem is so universal that it is not only the breeding ground for mental health disturbances such as anxiety, depression, and stress-related disorders, but it also often accounts for relationship problems and difficulties in school and work, resulting in social disconnectedness and loneliness. Furthermore, all the emotional and psychological effects take a toll on your physical health, even affecting your longevity. Conversely, the more unshakable your self-esteem, the more you will enjoy a happier, healthier, and fulfilling life.

The tips I offer in this book are based on evidence-based research from major psychological orientations, combining cognitive behavioral therapy (CBT) techniques with some newer "third wave" techniques. Third wave treatments combine Eastern-inspired mindfulness and acceptance strategies with traditionally Western CBT methods. In both CBT and third wave approaches, self-esteem is widely accepted as a cornerstone to mental health and wellness, and I have highlighted practical strategies from these approaches in this book.

I have been a psychotherapist in a variety of therapeutic settings, mostly in private practice. I have also provided continuing education programs for other mental health professionals on topics such as anxiety, mood disorders, personality disorders, and dealing with treatment-resistant clients. I have applied my therapeutic knowledge to the workplace as a motivational speaker at conferences, retreats, and trainings designed to increase positive communication and emotional health at home and at work. I have been struck by how much low self-esteem lies at the base of many personal, social, and workplace problems. I have also seen those who are more self-loving and self-accepting thrive in similar and even more challenging situations. This awareness moved me to write a book about embracing your greatness, because the more we think we are worthy and great, the greater will be our capacity for joy and happiness.

Aside from my experience as a clinician and speaker, I am the author of six mental health books. Most of them comprise my Tips and Tools for the Therapeutic Toolbox series, which offers practical, hands-on resources such as handouts and worksheets, along with activities for mental health clinicians to use with their clients to help with common issues.

Based on my own experience, and backed by concepts gleaned from research in the field as well as from studying current popular treatment trends, I offer this book to therapists, clients, and self-help enthusiasts who are looking for practical tips to overcome self-doubt and boost self-esteem. You will learn a variety of insights and practices that will improve the quality of your life *now.* Not *when* you are ten pounds lighter, *when* you are more successful, *when* you get that promotion, *when* you get in to your top-choice school, *when* you make more money, *when* your children finally get themselves together, or *when* you finally meet that special someone. Embracing your greatness is about loving yourself and your life *now* with no preconditions: no ifs, ands, or buts. It is about not waiting for things to change before you can be happy with yourself and your life. It is all about how to love yourself along your journey, without waiting for your world to change on the outside to feel better about who you are *right now.*

In each of the ten chapters in this book I have crystallized the most important keys to embracing your greatness. Each chapter consists of five tips, wherein I introduce a concept, follow it with relevant research or expert insights, and then offer an activity in the "Give It a Try" section. This practical focus will not only teach you *what* you can change, but it will show you *how to* change. Much like a recipe offers the ingredients to make a favorite dish followed by step-by-step instructions, the "Give It a Try" sections that follow each tip will map out practical steps for change.

This book will accommodate your preferred reading style. Some readers like to read a book from start to finish, while others like to pick it up and put it down for a quick read, choosing a topic that is relevant at the time without needing to have the background of preceding chapters. If you want to go directly to a topic that is particularly applicable to you at the time, you can scan the titles of the various sections to find what you need at the moment. Each of the five tips per chapter can stand alone, and each tip-plus-activity combination makes it easy to focus on and review select themes as you work on mastering the insights and skills that most pertain to you. However, for a greater grasp of the ten topics as a whole—of the breadth of ideas and activities per topic—I would recommend reading each chapter in its entirety at some point.

For the sections that are most relevant to you, you will find that revisiting them from time to time and repeating certain activities will be helpful. Repetition will be your friend as you develop new knowledge and habits. Just like you can't learn to play a musical instrument well by just taking lessons, developing new personal growth skills will require practice, practice, and more practice!

You will notice that many of the exercises that guide you through practicing these skills entail some writing—I want to explain here why written exercises have such enormous benefits:

- Writing things down on paper or on the computer helps you zero in on and eliminate unhealthy ways of thinking, replacing them with healthier alternatives. Unhealthy ways of thinking that are not well identified serve as an irritating backdrop in your life, like an annoying pebble in your shoe.

- By writing out your thoughts, you will gain the objectivity needed to change unhealthy perceptions into more positive and healthy thinking habits.

- Writing your thoughts down makes you face them. It makes your thoughts and issues tangible in the real world rather than in the recesses of your mind. When we keep them in our head, we tend to avoid them or treat them like just a nagging cold—not bad enough to justify taking drastic measures, but never really getting rid of them either.

- Writing down your thoughts helps you gain a different perspective on them. Problems become more solvable. Just like with many math or physics equations, some problems are just too complex to figure out in your head. But doing the "longhand" work to get them "out there" can help you better resolve complicated issues.

- Writing things down keeps you focused on the problem. When they stay only in our heads, we tend to get distracted and not address them once and for all. They end up being background scenery for our lives instead of issues to be addressed and tackled front and center.

As you read this book and do the accompanying written assignments, consider keeping a journal to help record and process your learning as you proceed. Journaling is an important tool for self-discovery and processing, and it helps us cope with painful memories, secrets, or factors that hold us back. Psychologist Ed Bourne (2010) cites many psychological and even physical benefits of what he calls "compassionate journaling," which honors our pain through focusing on developing self-compassion, helping us to reaffirm our self-worth and self-acceptance in our journaling.

So are you ready to learn how to get the life you want and deserve? If so, here's what to expect from this book:

- It is about getting rid of the obstacles that get in your way of really, really loving yourself and being your own best friend.

- It is about squashing the preoccupation about how you goofed, should have known better, or somehow should be different than you already are.

- It is about taking inventory of your beauty and greatness more than you take inventory of your flaws, mistakes, and regrets.

- It is about viewing your shortcomings with compassion and your future with hope and optimism.

- It is about learning from the past rather than wallowing in it.

- It is about living mindfully in the present, with an eye optimistically on the future.

- It is about taking care of yourself in mind, body, and spirit.

- It is about finding your own voice and standing up for yourself.

- It is about learning tools to change and develop new patterns of thinking and behaving.

- It is about using stress to challenge and motivate rather than to debilitate.

- It is about being strong enough to risk appearing weak by asking for help and enlisting support.

- It is about rewriting your life story to one of courage, faith, and resiliency.

- It is about focusing not on what you have lost, but more importantly, on what you have left.

Don't you deserve to be happy and love yourself once and for all—as you are *right now*? Let's learn some practical strategies that will help you to embrace your greatness and build truly unshakable self-esteem!

Embrace Your Self~Worth

OVERCOMING LOW SELF-ESTEEM

L ow self-esteem is one of the most common issues that underlie the majority of emotional and mental health problems, and it is one of the most common reasons why people seek therapy. It is a foundation from which many mental health disorders arise, including anxiety, depression, addictions, attention-deficit/ hyperactivity disorder, and relationship problems. Low self-esteem has robbed countless individuals of feeling true joy, negatively affecting virtually all aspects of life. Low self-esteem can rob us of our confidence in ourselves and our ability to feel good about who we are. It not only permeates our feelings about ourselves, but it handicaps our ability to relate to the world around us and it negatively impacts our relationships, work, attitudes, choices, physical health, and even life span.

You can think of low self-esteem as the common cold of emotional disturbance. Low self-esteem and self-dislike lie at the source of most mental health disorders. Cognitive behavioral therapy founder Aaron Beck (1972) found a strong link between self-criticism and depression, with up to 80 percent of depressed individuals reporting low self-evaluation. He cited a solid correlation between the sense of "self-deficiency" and the degree of depression. Low self-esteem is also strongly correlated with anxiety, eating disorders, ADHD, addictions, and other various difficulties.

Despite the far reach of low self-esteem in our lives, unlike depression and anxiety and other common mental health problems, there is no pill to treat it and it is not an official mental health diagnosis. The degree of self-esteem we have is dependent on a combination of our genetic predisposition and our environment. Maybe your parents, albeit unintentionally, communicated that your bad behavior meant that you were a bad person. Maybe you had trouble being accepted by peers and might even have been bullied or rejected. Maybe you were the victim of emotional, verbal, physical, or sexual abuse. Maybe you simply never received unconditional support and validation because the people around you, even if they meant well, were not healthy enough to give it to you. Or maybe you were just hardwired to be exquisitely sensitive and anxious, leading you to feeling out of sync with the rest of the world and causing you to doubt yourself and your worth.

Improving self-esteem requires the delicate balance of acknowledging the pain of the past while refusing to give the past more power than the present. The focus shifts from reliving and revisiting the past to learning, healing, and growing from it. Acknowledging past hurts rather than suppressing them is crucial to being free from them, whereas reliving them gets us stuck there. It's a tough balancing act to open your wounds in order to heal, much like a cut needs to be cleaned and treated, without picking too much at the scab and making things worse.

Learning new skills and altering perceptions help us get past the past. The important thing to keep reminding yourself is that self-esteem is alterable and is something you can change *now*. Whether it is shaky or unshakable depends on how much you choose to love yourself instead of judge yourself. Low self-esteem does not need to be a life sentence. Regardless of our genetic wiring, our interpretations that we choose to make about ourselves now will determine how the rest of our lives go. We potentially can have much more power over our thoughts than we realize. It comes down to learning to take charge of your life, reframing your perceptions, and developing new techniques to claim the self-love that you deserve.

It might take some work to embrace your greatness, but aren't you worth it?

1: Take Stock of Your Self-Esteem

"A man cannot be comfortable without his own approval."

—Mark Twain

When I think of self-love, I think of Whitney Houston's 1986 hit song "The Greatest Love of All," which regards the most important love of all to be our own self-love. It seems so intuitive that if we love ourselves, we are more likely to love our lives. It's almost impossible to be happy if we are not happy with ourselves. When we love ourselves unconditionally, we are more likely to experience positivity and are open to growth and new experiences. We are able to meet new situations with confidence and enthusiasm. No amount of love that anyone else shows us will be as crucial to our self-view as the love we are able to give ourselves.

You can think of living a life of self-confidence, growth, and resiliency as living life in *change mode,* which is when we embrace growth and change, feel free to be ourselves, are okay with making mistakes, and learn from setbacks rather than being defined by them. However, if you have learned or if you even perceived early on that the world is not a safe, validating place, you will carry a sense of fear and distrust well into adulthood.

When you are limited by fears and self-doubt, it is as if you are operating in *survival mode*. The goal of being in survival mode is not to grow and adapt to change; rather, this mode of living is designed to merely "get by"—by not making mistakes, not upsetting the proverbial apple cart with others, not taking any missteps that can lead to rejection or criticism from others. It becomes all about self-preservation and safety.

If you have been a victim of emotional, verbal, or physical abuse or neglect, the wounds run particularly deep, leaving you to see the world as unsafe and even downright scary. For example, if you felt like you needed to be "under the radar" during childhood to avoid getting "in trouble," that protective behavior will prove harmful later in life when trying to build closeness and intimacy in your relationships. When you function in survival mode instead of change mode, your distrust of others and your fear of change are really extensions of a lack of confidence in yourself. Keeping up a protective shell will handicap all areas of your life.

How about you? Have you been spending too much time in survival mode instead of change mode? Have you been waiting a long time to get your life to fall into place? Do you find yourself being held back by triggers from the past? If you find yourself agreeing with any of these questions, then are you ready to learn practical skills and techniques that can help you transform your life *now*?

GIVE IT A TRY

For each of the areas of self-esteem that follow, rate how you score right now on a scale of 1 to 10. After you add up all your ratings in your journal, divide that number by 10 and locate your score on the numerical scale below. The higher the number, the more it reflects healthy self-worth and self-empowerment. Conversely, the lower the score, the more it shows that you are *surviving* instead of *thriving*.

1	2	3	4	5	6	7	8	9	10

Do Not Agree   **Moderately Agree**   **Strongly Agree**

_____ I like myself and feel worthy.

_____ I do not expect perfection and am tolerant of my imperfections and even failures.

_____ I tend to think rationally and optimistically; I am able to distinguish between what is my perception and what is objective fact.

_____ I tend to learn from the past rather than live in it; I refuse to live life in the rearview mirror.

_____ Instead of being self-critical or hard on myself, I treat myself with the kindness and compassion that I would show to a loved one.

_____ I live present-focused and mindfully with non-judgmental awareness, rather than being focused on my ruminations of the past and anxieties about the future.

_____ I have good self-care habits and make my health in mind and body a priority.

_____ I feel free to express myself with confidence and honesty, without fear of the disapproval or criticism of others.

_____ I have supportive relationships, am forgiving, and enjoy giving to others.

_____ I am resilient and positive, and I love myself and love my life.

How did you do? In what areas do you experience the highest levels of success, and what areas need more work? Each of the ten statements above correspond, in order, to the ten chapters of this book. So if you want to get right to work on the issues that are the most problematic for you, you can start off reading those chapters on the areas where you scored the lowest. The lower your score in each item, the more skill building you need for that topic. The higher your score in each category, the more you are able to enjoy the freedom to be yourself, love yourself, and embrace your greatness with unshakable self-esteem!

2: Understand the Importance of Self-Esteem

"No one can make you feel inferior without your consent."

—Eleanor Roosevelt

Self-esteem is crucial to our ability to truly like ourselves. The lower our self-esteem, the more we tend to get depressed and anxious and to experience other emotional and physical problems. When we don't like ourselves enough, we tend to be hypersensitive to perceived rejection, and we're more likely to take the comments of others as criticism. The less confidence you have, the more you will seek validation and approval from others at the expense of seeking your own approval.

When you tend to search for reassuring signs from others that you are okay, you are not focusing on the real issue, which is getting *you* to think you are okay. You can't get from others what you need to develop inside you—after all, self-esteem is an inside job. Ironically, the more you fear rejection and are needy for approval, the more you feel alone, isolated, and alienated from others. Giving others power over your self-esteem is a no-win proposition.

Even when we feel temporarily pleased with ourselves and think that things are going well, those with low self-esteem are just waiting for the other shoe to drop. The temporary high we feel upon getting approval from others pales in comparison to the fear of not getting it the next time or, worse yet, receiving outright rejection. Neediness for approval is a setup for depression and anxiety.

Lisa Schaub, in *The Self-Esteem Workbook for Teens* (2013), reminds us that although we might feel defective, when we are born there are not two nurseries—one for worthless babies and one for valuable ones. Rather, all babies are placed in the same room and are equally valuable. Regrettably, some of us forget our worth and believe the lies we tell ourselves that we are not as worthy. Schaub makes the point that there is no doctor that would tell the parents of a newborn baby things like, *"This baby is not as good as others"* or *"This child is inferior."* She makes the case that you believing you are not good enough and unworthy is just as preposterous as this absurd scenario. We don't transform from being a worthy, precious human being into an unworthy one—our worth is intact no matter what.

Healthy self-esteem gives us the confidence to believe that even if things do not turn out well, we still can. Are you ready to believe in that beautiful person who is you?

GIVE IT A TRY

This exercise will tap into the power of seeing yourself as a precious being.

Step 1: Think for a moment of how you came into the world: a beautiful baby who was precious, valuable, and whole. Along the way maybe you received negative messages from your caregivers, siblings, or other family members, peers, teachers, and so forth, who did not give you the support you needed. Even those with the best intentions might not have been able to give you noncritical messages in order to teach you and shape you, leaving you with the impression that you were "unlikable" or "bad" when they corrected you. Think of any negative takeaways you have gotten and look at them now with fresh eyes.

Step 2: Write those messages down and look at them objectively. *Were* they true? *Are* they true? Or were those takeaways really more of a reflection of others, not you? For example, if you were teased at school for being unpopular, unattractive, or stupid, was the bullying reflective of you or of those who bullied you?

Step 3: If you happen to have photos of yourself as a baby, choose one to look at and study how beautiful and precious you were. If you do not have a photo, imagine yourself as a baby or look at a picture of a baby and imagine it is you. Hopefully, you will see the beauty in you as a small child.

Step 4: Now draw an image of yourself as a child. Art ability is not necessary—this is not a time to be critical of your drawing ability. It is an exercise to draw yourself with a fresh perspective, symbolically recreating your view of yourself in a fresh light.

Step 5: As you look at your drawing, think of the messages you received—and still receive—that you are not good enough, smart enough, attractive enough, or likable enough. How many of those messages now come from you? With each negative thought or critical message from yourself or others, rip off a small or large piece of your drawing. With each thought that undermines your self-esteem, rip off another piece and observe yourself literally tearing yourself apart! Reflect on how much of the paper is left at the end of this exercise. This represents the fragment of the remaining self-esteem that you are walking around with.

Step 6: Now think of how you can put back some of the pieces—such as with tape—with the perspective, knowledge, and support you can enlist. However torn you feel, this is the time to heal and make yourself whole again. Symbolically, piece the pieces of your self-esteem back together, with kinder messages to replace the old destructive ones.

What messages can you now tell yourself that would make you feel whole again? It is up to you now to make sure you do not allow your own inner dialogue or the words or actions of others to further tear you down or tear you up. You are worthy no matter what. Don't you deserve to feel whole?

3: Make Self-Esteem Unconditional

"Self-esteem is the greatest sickness known to man or woman because it's conditional."

—Albert Ellis

Although no one would argue against the importance of self-esteem, *how we get it* determines if it is healthy self-esteem or just basically a setup for misery. If we get our self-esteem by comparing ourselves to others, we'll face a lifetime of problems, for we may feel superior in some ways, at some times, but we'll feel inferior just as often—we'll always find others who excel more in any given area or have something we lack.

It is therefore crucial to differentiate *conditional* self-esteem, which is based on being successful and feeling better than others, from *unconditional* self-esteem, which is based on a solid, internal sense of self-worth. Unfortunately, much of what we are taught about self-esteem is that we need to be above average, excel, and succeed in order to earn self-worth. The problem is that when we feel temporarily good about ourselves when we excel, we are setting ourselves up for disliking ourselves when we don't make the mark and find ourselves below average. Not everyone can get straight A's in life. Basing your self-worth on achievements, likability, and successes and disliking yourself when you don't make the mark are just two sides of the same coin. When your feelings about yourself are based on anything conditional, like whether or not you stand out from the crowd, you are doomed to be generally unhappy.

In simple terms, self-esteem that correlates to what we *do* rather than who we *are* can be problematic, especially if it is based on how you fare compared to others. Conditional self-esteem feels great when we do well, but it leaves us in the dust when we don't. Conditional self-esteem is there when we succeed, but it deserts us when we fall short. Just when we need it the most, it leaves us. This reminds me of a Randy VanWarmer song from the '70s about the aftermath of a breakup, "Just When I Needed You Most." It was a popular song about unrequited love, but I see this ballad poignantly reflecting the pain of deserting yourself in tough times—just when you need yourself the most. During times when you need self-acceptance, all too often those with low self-esteem use setbacks as another excuse for self-flagellation.

The founder of acceptance and commitment therapy (ACT), Steven Hayes (2005), offers some practical solutions to improve our ability to be more self-accepting. ACT is a relatively new treatment approach that has become quite popular and has given us a wealth of visualizations to help us work on acceptance of ourselves instead of basing our worthiness on other people's opinions of us or our performance.

How do you derive your self-esteem? Is it too conditional? Do you have a hard time accepting yourself, flaws and all? If so, isn't it time to start loving yourself unconditionally and treating yourself with the respect you deserve?

GIVE IT A TRY

Here are three visualizations adapted from ACT that can help you learn the art of accepting yourself without judgment.

Step 1: Read these three visualizations and personalize how these symbolic images can help you alter your own self-view and increase your self-acceptance.

> **Quicksand Visualization:** When you struggle to get out of quicksand, you sink in deeper. Likewise, when you try to stop or resist your thoughts, that often makes things worse. Picture quicksand when you catch yourself trying to be like someone else, be the best, or gain the approval of others. Instead of sinking further into this trap of nonacceptance, ask yourself, *What would my life be like if I found more value in who I am rather than resisting who I am?*
>
> **Passengers on the Bus Visualization:** Imagine you are driving a bus, going toward a personal goal, such as developing the ability to accept and love yourself. There are cranky passengers on the bus representing your judgmental and critical thoughts about yourself, sabotaging your goal of self-acceptance by saying things like, *"You're unlikable," "You're not good enough," "You're just stupid," "You're fat," "You're ugly."* Visualize yourself refusing to listen to them and instead look straight ahead with your eyes fixed on your goal of reaching the land of self-acceptance and self-love. You as the driver have the power to refuse to listen to those critical messages

distracting you from the goal of self-acceptance. *On the road to self-love, you are in the driver's seat!*

Thought Train Visualization: Picture yourself on a bridge, watching a train, and each boxcar on the train has a critical or negative thought about yourself written on it. For example, one car might have *I am not likable* on it, and another might have *I should be smarter.* As you watch the train go by, distance yourself from those thoughts rather than identify with them. The more you develop an "observing head" to those thoughts, the less you believe them. As you watch your negative thoughts about yourself from a distance, you can see them without getting too attached to them.

Step 2: Ask yourself these questions to process the visualizations:

- *What thoughts did I use for these visualizations?*

- *What would life be like if I gained some distance from my self-doubting thoughts?*

- *What unhelpful thoughts keep sidetracking me, and what personal goals can help me stay on track?*

Step 3: Taking at least one of the visualizations that you find most helpful, select a metaphorical object that symbolizes that visualization to keep in a visible place, such as at your desk, in your car, or on your kitchen counter. For instance, a toy train can serve as a reminder to just watch your negative thoughts go by you on a train as you distance yourself from those thoughts.

Instead of letting yourself get sidetracked, isn't it about time to commit yourself to your own path, accept your flaws, and trust in your journey?

4: Learn a New Emotional Language to Improve Self-Esteem

*"Everything can be taken from a man but one thing:
the last of the human freedoms—to choose one's
attitude in any given set of circumstances."*

—Viktor Frankl

I have often been struck by the fact that no matter when people emigrate from one country to another, their accents often stay with them. No matter how proficient they are in their acquired language, the accent from their home country is still strong even decades later. The accent remains unmistakable no matter how long a person lives in the new country. This demonstrates how strongly influenced we are by our mother tongue, the first language we learn.

I liken that concept to how we learn our basic emotional language. In an effort to help us sort out our feelings from our thoughts and behaviors, and to demonstrate how changing and disputing thoughts can change your feelings and behaviors, psychologist Albert Ellis's ABC model (sometimes extrapolated to ABCDE) can be a very valuable tool to change our language of emotion, which in turn can boost our self-esteem. First developed in the 1950s, the model has remained a popular technique to challenge esteem-bashing self-talk.

Here is the basic ABC model:

A = Activating Event: This is the situation that causes emotional upset and triggers self-doubt and possible unhealthy behaviors and choices.

B = Beliefs: Beliefs underlie upsetting emotions. Therefore, if your thinking is distorted or unhealthy, then your feelings and behaviors will be unhealthy too. Take the example of a relationship breakup: the breakup itself does not cause you to feel worthless; rather, it is your *thoughts* about the breakup that determine how you see yourself and how you cope. In essence, no one "makes us devastated" or drives us to drink—our thoughts do!

C = Consequences (Feelings and Behaviors): Now, what are the emotions and resulting behaviors that stem from your beliefs about the activating event? For example, depression, anxiety, sadness, and anger are all examples of upsetting emotions, and sample behaviors reacting to those feelings include using food and alcohol in excess to help you cope or using recreational drugs.

D = Dispute the Irrational Thoughts: After crystallizing the thoughts that lead to self-defeating emotions and behaviors, it is time to challenge those thoughts with questions like, *Where is the evidence that the belief is true? Aren't I just as worthy even if I am alone?*

E = Effect of Disputing Irrational Thoughts: Disputing irrational thoughts results in healthier and more positive emotions and behaviors. For example, despite sadness over the loss of the relationship, you will not use the breakup as an opportunity to put yourself down or beat yourself up, and thus the event will not lead to self-sabotaging behaviors such as excessive eating or drinking.

How about you? Are you ready to give up your unhealthy emotional language to really love and accept yourself? Isn't it time to let go of the emotional barriers that hold you back?

GIVE IT A TRY

Use the psychological ABC framework to look at your own experience.

Step 1: Take a few moments to imagine how your life would be different if you were more aware of the B's (beliefs) that fall between your A's (activating or actual events) and your C's (consequences). With practice, you will be more in control of how events affect you, as you become more aware of the thoughts that exist between outside events and how you feel and react to them. When you dispute your thoughts, you learn to challenge unhealthy ways of thinking—you can literally change your thoughts to change your life! Even though this ABC model seems like a simple formula, it takes a lot of practice to get it right! In learning a new language, practice is the key.

Step 2: Consider keeping a daily ABC diary for at least a few weeks, with a minimum of one or two entries a day. Just like with learning a new language, developing a workout routine, or studying a new subject, trying something only once or twice will not help you make meaningful progress. As you use this model regularly—putting into writing your own ABCDE's—you will train yourself to be a better "thought catcher."

It's never too late to learn another language. Don't you deserve to take charge of your thoughts and feelings and take control of your life?

5: Live in the Land of Good Enough

"I was most terrified of not being enough. Not being good enough, pretty enough, skinny enough."

—Oprah Winfrey

There's a land that most people can only dream of. It's a land that can be so close to us, but at times it seems so far away. It's a land where we don't have to be ruled by a need to be perfect or even better than we are right now. It's a land in which worthiness is given to you—it does not have to be earned. It's a land where people strive to be genuine, kind, and authentic, where they are accepted for who they are, not what they do. It is a land where there are no expectations on how you "should be." It's a land where love is in the air and peace and joy abound. It's called the "land of good enough."

As shown by the above quote from an April 2017 interview in *People* magazine, even one of the most successful individuals on this planet, Oprah Winfrey, has struggled to be a citizen of the land of good enough. No wonder so many of us have such a hard time getting there! If this wildly accomplished woman has felt like she was never good enough, it's not a stretch in the least to question if most of us, without anywhere near the fame and fortune she enjoys, can ever make peace with being in that land!

The land of good enough is one that can offer you a safe harbor from competition and perfectionism. It is a place that is forgiving and that allows flaws and mistakes without judgment. *How Good Do We Have to Be?* author Harold Kushner (1997) laments that our society encourages us to think that if you are not the best, you have failed. He shared a story from his own life in which coming in second place in a national spelling bee was almost seen as a failure. As a young child, when he placed second in the contest, he was allowed to go into the "crying room." We can learn from this example the importance of becoming more self-accepting and less perfectionistic to prove our worth. When we can tackle this kind of all-or-nothing thinking and overcome perfectionism (the focus of the next chapter), we can embrace living in the land of good enough.

How about you? Do you think too much in terms of success or failure, looking for perfection rather than being happy with being in the "land of good enough"? If so, don't you want to start thinking in ways that will help you rather than hurt you? Are you ready to take control of your thoughts to take control of your life?

GIVE IT A TRY

As emphasized in the introduction to this book, writing assignments provide many benefits for processing and tackling the unhealthy all-or-nothing thinking that underlies low self-esteem.

Step 1: To identify if you are thinking in extreme, all-or-nothing ways, learn to separate unhealthy from healthy thoughts with this model below. Which column more accurately reflects your thinking style in times of adversity and stress?

All-or-Nothing Thinking	Rational, Healthy Thinking
It's terrible she said that!	*I was upset when she said that.*
I'll never get it right!	*I am having a hard time with this assignment.*
I'm a failure.	*I am good enough.*

Step 2: Create a page in your journal or on your computer that looks like the model above, with two column headings. Under the first, write down examples of your own all-or-nothing thoughts—think of at least three examples of unhealthy thinking that leads to low self-esteem. Then, under the second column, replace those statements with healthier, more rational thoughts. Notice how extreme all-or-nothing thinking makes you a victim, whereas rational, healthy thinking is factual and self-empowering.

Step 3: On file cards follow the same format—write *All-or-Nothing Thought* on one side and *Rational, Healthy Thought* on the other. Each time a negative, self-defeating thought arises throughout your day, write it down on a separate card, then flip it over and offer a healthier alternative. This is a variation of what are known as "coping cards," a cornerstone of major treatment approaches such as CBT. Carry your cards around with you to review periodically to help you develop a healthier mind-set.

Actively tackling your all-or-nothing ways of thinking will give you your best shot at loving yourself to love your life!

Embrace Your Imperfections

OVERCOMING PERFECTIONISM

Have you ever been afraid of making a mistake or being seen as "stupid" or "lame"? Are you riddled with anxiety about "messing up"? Do you think that if you "screw up" that makes you a failure? Are you constantly seeking approval from others at the cost of approving of yourself?

If you answer yes to any of these questions, then you suffer from emotionally crippling perfectionism. Perfectionism is one of the greatest self-esteem robbers. That is because perfectionism is not just trying to be your best. In fact, it is not about being you at all. Rather, it is all about how you think you *should be*. It is too focused on what other people think. It is all based on evaluation and judgment instead of on self-love and acceptance. When people are perfectionistic, they believe that unless they achieve certain standards, they are inadequate, defective, and—even worse—unworthy.

Perfectionism does not just affect your sense of well-being and your emotional health. Over time, anxious, perfectionistic thinking also takes a toll on your physical health, and is linked to a variety of illnesses and diseases including cancer, heart disease, gastrointestinal disorders, and immune system deficiencies. Mental illness such as depression, obsessive-compulsive disorder, and body dysmorphia is also an outgrowth of perfectionism.

David Burns, CBT psychologist and author, describes perfectionism as an impossible goal. According to Burns, a perfectionist is someone "whose standards are high beyond reach or reason" and "who strains compulsively and unremittingly toward impossible goals and who measures their own worth entirely in terms of productivity and accomplishment. For these people the drive to excel can only be self-defeating" (1980, 34).

How about you? Do you suffer from the need to be perfect? Do you find your goals too demanding and impossibly unreachable? Are you ready to learn how to shift from being perfect to embracing how to be perfectly *you*?

6: Overcome Perfectionism

"If you look for perfection, you'll never be content."
—Leo Tolstoy

I recall something a perfectionistic client who was a lab technician said to me many years back, which still haunts me today. When I asked her why she was so afraid of doing poorly at her job, she raised her hand high over my coffee table and poignantly explained, "I have had this many failures—and I can't afford one more." "Wow," I responded, "that's quite a large pile. Can you name some of them?" Interestingly enough, she could think of only two, but they loomed larger than life and defined her as a "failure."

Shame researcher Brené Brown (2010) draws a correlation between shame and perfectionism. She regards shame as the underlying driver of perfectionism. Shame and low self-esteem are exquisitely intertwined. At the root of shame is an all-pervasive sense of unworthiness, being unlikable and undeserving, seeing yourself as fundamentally flawed and even *bad*.

It is not unusual to confuse shame and guilt. Although too much guilt can lead to shame if self-flagellation becomes all-pervasive, guilt in itself is not unhealthy. Having a degree of guilt and remorse for having done something hurtful or wrong helps us to learn from our mistakes and propels us to behave better and correct unhealthy behavior. Shame, on the other hand, is never healthy. It does not push us to do better but makes us feel worse about ourselves and keeps us beaten down. When we feel a lack of self-worth and inherent badness, we feel shameful. It is not corrective and helpful; it destroys our love and respect for ourselves.

One approach I have personally found useful in working with clients who carry around too much shame is to help them differentiate healthy guilt from shame, guiding them to challenge their shame-based thinking and to transform those thoughts into goals for improvement.

Are you ready to give up shame-based thoughts that lead to all the "supposed to be" messages so that you can stop doubting yourself and embrace your greatness?

GIVE IT A TRY

Use this written exercise to differentiate shame from guilt. This will help you transform shame-based thinking into manageable goals.

Step 1: Write down at least five reasons why you feel shame. If you have low self-esteem, no doubt you tell yourself many critical and self-downing things.

Step 2: In looking at your list, ask yourself how many of your responses actually represent healthy guilt versus shame. Guilt might apply to actions you regret, such as blowing up at someone close to you, which can lead you to learn to control your anger and handle your frustration more assertively. With healthy guilt, it will be a prompt to healthier action, which helps you act better. With shame, self-worth is judged with faulty logic, such as *I did bad things, so I am a bad person.*

Step 3: With the items remaining that reflect shame, recognize how judgmental and all-pervasive your self-sabotaging statements are. To make you less immobilized by put-downs about yourself, write down actionable goals to improve your behaviors now. To do this, create three columns. In the first column write your guilt-ridden, shame-based statement. In the second column write the perfectionistic takeaway based on that thought. In the third column create an actionable step to turn shame into healthier goals you can control. For example:

Shame-Based Thought	Perfectionistic Takeaway	Turn Thoughts into Goals
I'm such a loser.	*I am afraid to speak up at the meeting as I don't want to be wrong and make any more mistakes.*	*I will speak up at least once in each meeting. Even if I say something I regret, it doesn't mean I'm stupid.*

Step 4: Looking at what you wrote in column three, take a moment to imagine how your life would be different if you turned your perfectionistic self-talk into goals. How does it feel shifting from perfectionism, which is problem-focused, to goals, which are solution-focused?

Instead of getting stuck in unresolvable problems from the past, what steps are you going to take to move into the future with a more action-oriented and positive view? Aren't you worth it?

7: Quell the Inner Critic

"You've been criticising yourself for years and it hasn't worked. Try approving of yourself and see what happens."

—Louise Hay

If you have low self-esteem, your inner critic sure knows how to push your buttons and pull your triggers. Your inner critic has way too much power over you, more than anything or anybody else. Whose voice are you hearing, anyway? Are you listening to critical and judgmental parents or others at home or at school who were not healthy enough to provide you with a nonjudgmental and supportive foundation? Did you grow up with the message that when you didn't act the way they wanted you to, you were bad or unlovable? Were you not given the assurance that even if you did bad things, you were not a bad person?

Even the most well-meaning parents and caregivers fall short in providing an atmosphere of what humanistic psychologist Carl Rogers (1956) called "unconditional positive regard." The intent is not to blame those important people in your life—no one chooses to be dysfunctional—but just to understand how those conditional and critical messages crippled our self-esteem. If you got the underlying message that you were not good enough or smart enough, you might have trouble seeing yourself as worthy and lovable. Maybe your caregivers early on did not realize that in trying to motivate you to excel and shape you to be better, they were inadvertently teaching you the wrong things—leading you to think you were not good enough already. And if you had the misfortune of being put down by peers at school, you might even to this day still agree with the names they called you.

Whoever you are listening to through the voice of your inner critic, it is time to stand up, revolt, and stop giving the critic so much power! Listening to your inner critic only robs you of your happiness and joy. Even though your inner critic might sound very convincing, keep in mind that it's all lies. All human beings, no matter how flawed, deserve respect—most importantly from themselves!

Haven't you paid too high a price by listening to your inner critic? Isn't it time to challenge those old recordings in your head and set yourself free from that damaging all-or-nothing thinking?

GIVE IT A TRY

This exercise will help you meet your inner critic squarely and stand up to it once and for all!

Step 1: Think for a moment about what your inner critic says to you, then write down those thoughts—whatever you hear the critical voice inside of you say. Be as honest as you can with yourself, and try to crystallize the unkind messages you tell yourself that keep you feeling bad.

Step 2: Recording yourself on your smartphone, computer, or other device, read your inner critic's words aloud. Feel free to go off script and ham it up. Don't mince words—say exactly what's on the critic's mind!

Step 3: Listen to this recording over and over again until you become less fascinated and even bored with the inner critic's complaints about you. Once you get those thoughts out in the open and they stop circulating endlessly in your head, you can be more objective about the absurdity of those shaming messages— you will take away their power. Observe them rather than believe them unconditionally.

Step 4: After you listen to these self-downing messages over and over until they seem less potent, take each critical statement one by one and refute them. For each negative belief, challenge why your inner critic is wrong.

Step 5: Now write statements that are self-affirming and self-loving to counter those critical messages. For example, statements like *I'm a failure* and *Others are better than me* can be challenged with *Although I am human and make mistakes, that does not make me a failure* and *I am just as worthy as everyone else.* Tone down the dramatic thinking.

Step 6: Just as you did for the unhealthy messages, record yourself reading aloud the healthier, refuting statements. Then listen to those healthier statements repeatedly until you believe them! Don't they sound better? Aren't they much kinder? You might even want to try saying them to yourself in the mirror a few times a day until you no longer give your inner critic so much power over you.

The way you choose to see yourself now is truly a choice. Isn't it time to stop listening to those ancient tapes in your head and replace them with kinder ones?

8: Give Yourself Permission to Fail

> *"Failure is simply the opportunity to begin again, this time more intelligently."*
>
> —Henry Ford

What do Michael Jordan, Abraham Lincoln, Walt Disney, Thomas Edison, Babe Ruth, the Beatles, Oprah Winfrey, and Richard Branson have in common? They are all famous and considered to be some of the greatest success stories in history. However, you might not know that all of them also experienced extreme failure:

- In 1923 Babe Ruth not only set the home run record of the season, he also set the record for the most strikeouts.

- Michael Jordan was cut from his high school basketball team.

- Oprah Winfrey was fired from her first TV reporting job and was told she was not cut out for television since she was too emotional.

- Walt Disney was fired at age twenty-two from a Missouri newspaper because he was not considered to be "creative enough."

- The Beatles were rejected by Decca Records in 1962.

- Abraham Lincoln had a succession of failures, including losing his family farm, being demoted from a captain to a private in the army, failing as a storekeeper, and losing multiple bids for Congress, the Senate, and the vice presidency.

- Billionaire Richard Branson, founder of Virgin Records and Virgin Airlines, lost millions and even billions of dollars in failed business ventures, including Virgin Cola, Virgin Cars, Virgin Digital (music downloads), and Virgin Brides (wedding boutiques).

- Thomas Edison was fired from his first two jobs and tried one thousand ways to make a lightbulb before finally succeeding.

Why are so many of us so afraid of failure? This list makes plain that many successful people have failed. In fact, their failures were necessary precursors to their successes. If you don't try, you won't be able to succeed. All too often we are so afraid of failing that we never give ourselves the chance to succeed and learn from our errors. Perfectionists are notorious for trying to avoid failure at all costs. The problem is, when we avoid failure like the plague, we also avoid the potential to build on our failures and succeed.

The important issue is not whether you fail, but how you respond to your failures. So how about learning from famous examples and giving yourself a chance to succeed?

GIVE IT A TRY

Learning to build upon failures instead of being defined by them will help you grow from them and move forward.

Step 1: Think of people in your own life. Do you know anyone who has failed at something but was resilient enough to forge ahead and pave the way for more success? What can you learn from them? Do you admire them for their resilience, or are you focused more on their failures? Chances are you look at their failures more kindly than your own. When we are perfectionistic, we are our own worst critics and are much more accepting of the shortcomings of others.

Step 2: Compose a list of your own failures, setbacks, or mistakes. Write out how they have they affected your view of yourself and how they have affected your life. Write down what you say to yourself about these mistakes and failures.

Step 3: Read this list of mistakes as if they were made by a close friend or valued family member. How would you see these setbacks differently if they were not your own? What would you say to your loved one about them? Imagine you are talking to your friend or family member and trying to soothe them—what words would you use?

Step 4: Looking in the mirror, say those words to yourself. Look yourself in the eye and give yourself words of comfort. Talk to yourself as if you were your best friend. Remind yourself that you are no less worthy than anyone else. You might want to create some affirmations or words of support that you can repeat to yourself throughout the day to help stay positive, such as *"I deserve to have a good day"* and *"I'm proud of who I am."*

Commit to building yourself up instead of beating yourself up. How long will you sentence yourself for mistakes made in your past if you are doing your best to be better now? Don't you deserve a second chance?

9: Stand Up to the Perfection Bully

"If you are a perfectionist, you are guaranteed to be a loser in whatever you do."

—David D. Burns

If you are fighting perfectionism, it might help to think of it as just a big bully. Your perfectionistic bully inside your head bosses you around, distorts your thinking, and makes you feel small and inadequate. The bully has standards that are illogical, harsh, critical, and unfair. Being intimidated by your inner bully is like being a child bullied at school—you lose your confidence and feel powerless. Yet you alone have the ability to stop listening to the bully and giving the bully so much power. As the saying goes, you don't need to keep renting out space in your head!

The best antidote to perfectionism is to identify and challenge what are called "cognitive distortions"—this process is one of the most widely used techniques in CBT and it will figure prominently throughout this book. We've already addressed a couple of distortions, as in all-or-nothing thinking, and now we'll expand our understanding of the concept with a fuller list of examples. Here are the types of cognitive distortions that particularly relate to perfectionism:

- **Black-and-White Thinking:** extreme all-or-nothing thinking that distorts logic and blows things out of proportion; evidenced in such words as "failed," "loser," "always," and "never."

- **Labeling:** being very judgmental and resorting to name-calling; not sticking to the facts by using words like "idiot" and "lazy."

- **Fortune-Telling:** believing you can tell the future, as if there is no hope for change; signaled by a phrase such as "I'll never…"

- **Emotional Reasoning:** gloomy interpretations based on negative emotions instead of objectivity.

- **Jumping to Conclusions:** erroneously tying two thoughts together; believing that "this happened, therefore that will happen."

- **Should Statements:** perfectionistic and critical expectations of how you "should" be.

- **Overgeneralization:** drawing generalized conclusions from a specific situation, such that one case of failure leads you to conclude that failure describes your whole identity.

- **Discounting the Positive:** using tunnel vision to discredit or ignore any other positive interpretation or outcome.

Take a sample statement from a perfectionist: *"I failed again—I'm just a loser who should be a lot further along in my life right now. I'll never get my life together!"* These examples demonstrate virtually all of the types of cognitive distortions listed above. Learning how to understand and combat your own cognitive distortions is vital to eliminating self-doubt.

Isn't it time to stand up to your inner bully that tells you such mean things? Isn't it time to think in shades of gray instead of black and white?

GIVE IT A TRY

Identifying and challenging your cognitive distortions will be one of the most important factors in eliminating self-doubt and embracing yourself, flaws and all.

Step 1: Using some of the perfectionistic thoughts you've already identified in previous sections of this chapter (or using new ones), write them down and then determine the cognitive distortion(s) that applies to each. Which distortions are the most persistent in your thought patterns? Which self-statements are the most disturbing to you?

Step 2: Now exaggerate your cognitive distortions (which are already distorted enough!) even further. Visualize your inner bully talking to you, really ratcheting up your cognitive distortions to the point of absurdity—maybe even in front of a mirror.

The idea is that if you exaggerate your fear, it will lose its power over you since it is obviously *so* distorted. For example, if you fear you are not going to succeed after a recent job promotion, you can dramatize those fears by saying, *"You are the worst supervisor who has ever lived on this planet!"* or *"You didn't even deserve this promotion in the first place—surely you'll be out of a job in a month or two!"*

Step 3: Visualizing the absurdity of your distortions can be eye-opening, but for more impact try a role-play with another person—a friend, family member, or therapist—acting the part of your inner bully, asking them to really ham it up! You'll likely end up laughing at how ridiculous your exaggerated fears seem when you actually hear them spoken aloud by someone else.

So how about putting your inner bully in its place and doubting the bully instead of doubting yourself? Remember, you don't have to believe everything you think!

10: Give Up Who You "Should Be"

"Stop shoulding on yourself."

—Albert Ellis

Do you spend too much time thinking of who you "should be" rather than appreciating who you are? Do you think you "should be" smarter, thinner, more attractive, more successful, have a better personality, or be better liked? Do you think that you "should" have a better house, a nicer car, better friends, smarter kids? Do you tend to review your past mistakes and find yourself "shoulding" on yourself for decisions, choices, and actions you now regret? Are you plagued with the sense that you "should" just plain be in a better place in your life by now?

If you answer yes to any of these questions, your "shoulds" are weighing you down and robbing you of your self-esteem and happiness. There is no shortage of the types of "should statements" that squash our self-esteem. Whether they focus on our sense of inadequacy about who we are compared to who we want to be, on our past mistakes, regretful decisions, or what we lack in our lives, our "shoulds" get in the way of self-acceptance and self-love. "Should" statements are inflexible, perfectionistic, and demanding.

Why not stop the guilt-tripping and put an end to your unreasonable "shoulds" starting today?

GIVE IT A TRY

By challenging our irrational beliefs about who or what we should be, we can be more authentically ourselves instead of some idealized, unattainable version of ourselves.

Step 1: Write down a list of your unrealistic expectations of yourself. You can start your statements with:

- *I should be…*

- *I should have been…*

- *I should have…*

- *I should get…*

- *I should always…*

- *I should never…*

Step 2: Looking at your list, ask yourself these questions:

- *Are these statements feasible?*

- *Are they even true?*

- *Where did I get these ideas?*

- *Am I listening to someone other than myself?*

- *Who am I really trying to please?*

What do you notice about your answers? Identify and write down what underlying assumptions are at the core of those statements. For example, if your reason behind the statement *I should be more successful by now* is that you are inferior to your friends or siblings who have more financial success, then address this fundamental problem of comparing yourself to others to rate your own self-worth.

Step 3: Now change the should statement into a more flexible and factual statement that replaces your rigid ideas with choices and preferences that help you strive to be the best you can be without comparing yourself to others:

- *I should be thinner* becomes *I would like to lose weight.*

- *I should never have taken that job* becomes *I made the best choice at the time and will review the options I have now.*

- *I should always know the right answers when I speak up in meetings* becomes *I will answer as best I can, realizing that it is okay to not know everything.*

Step 4: Consider putting these should statements in a "should jar." In my counseling office I have a jar labeled SHOULDS. Many clients over the years have brought in note cards or strips of paper with their should statements written on them to put in my jar as a symbolic gesture to get all their unrealistic expectations of themselves out of their heads! How about making your own receptacle where you can get all of your "shoulds" out of your head so you can get into your life?

Aren't you tired of being weighed down by all of those "shoulds" that rob you of realizing how great you are? Isn't it time to give them up so you can be authentically you?

Embrace Healthy Thinking

CHANGING YOUR THOUGHTS TO CHANGE YOUR LIFE

Did you know that if you change your thoughts, you literally could change your life? Most people do not realize that it is the way we think that determines our degree of happiness. Most people look for happiness outside of themselves, but nothing really ends up making us happy if we are not thinking clearly between our ears.

Despite the seemingly romantic '60s song made popular by Blood, Sweat & Tears, "You Make Me So Very Happy," happiness is really an inside job. No one can do that for you. Sure, people can *help* you to be happy, but the keys to our happiness lie within us, not in people or things outside of ourselves. Other people do help us considerably, but if you have negative self-perceptions and live life on the defensive, it's unlikely you will be very happy no matter how many people think you're great. So a more accurate song title would be "I'm So Very Happy Being with You." Maybe it wouldn't be as catchy, but it would be a lot more accurate!

This chapter will expand upon the cognitive behavioral therapy approaches we've touched on so far and draw on rational emotive behavior therapy (REBT) to identify your feelings, separate them from your thoughts, and learn skills to change your thoughts to change your life. Albert Ellis laid the foundation of REBT in the 1950s, and a decade later Aaron Beck initially developed CBT in his work on understanding the origins of depression (1967). CBT has become the most widely embraced therapeutic orientation in the Western world—perhaps the entire world. This orientation has helped millions of people with symptoms of low self-esteem, depression, and anxiety challenge their thinking habits to feel better and lead happier lives.

How about you? Are you ready to embrace the time-tested teachings from the great thinkers in the field of psychotherapy to change your thoughts to change your life?

11: Differentiate Thoughts
from Feelings

"You feel the way you do right now because of the thoughts you are thinking at this moment."

—David D. Burns

After months of looking for a new job after having been let go from his former position, thirty-six-year-old Douglas felt a mixture of excitement and dread his first week back to work at a new company. Feelings of relief were mixed with fears of losing this job too. The emotions he expressed were all over the place:

"I feel like maybe I can't handle this job!"

"I feel I am going to fail."

"I feel like they'll expect more than I can handle."

"I feel like they will think I am not as good as I seemed at my interview."

What do you notice about these statements? Douglas is stating his fears and perceptions as if they were absolute facts. He is confusing truth with the stories he tells himself based on his self-doubts and fears. In other words, Douglas's statements confuse thoughts and feelings. Despite the fact that all his sentences start with "I feel," those statements are not really feelings at all—*they are thoughts!* Underlying those thoughts are feelings of anxiety, fear, and panic. For example, the first statement in the list—*"I feel like maybe I can't handle this job!"*—erroneously confuses thoughts and feelings. A more factual restatement would be: *"I am afraid I won't do as well as they expect, and I am anxious about that."*

In *The Self-Esteem Workbook*, Glenn Schiraldi (2001) views "making feelings facts" as a type of distorted thinking that leads to low self-esteem. The example he gives—*"I feel inadequate. I must be inadequate"*—shows the illogical reasoning of feelings being seen as factual conclusions.

So why is it so important to clarify thoughts from feelings? If you can't tell them apart, you have no control over your moods. You can't convince yourself not to feel a certain way, but you can challenge unhealthy thinking and convince yourself to try healthier ways of thinking, which in turn will help you feel better. You can learn to control your moods by identifying and controlling your thoughts.

When we get better at differentiating thoughts from feelings, we literally change our lives from the inside out by taking control of the thoughts that lead to difficult emotions. Can you appreciate how your life can be different if you are able to separate your thoughts from your feelings?

GIVE IT A TRY

Separating thoughts from feelings can be a learned skill if you take the following steps.

Step 1: Identify a difficult situation in your own life that causes you anxiety and emotional pain. Write down at least three feelings related to this situation that you would like to change. Ask yourself, *Are these feelings or thoughts?* For example, if you write, *I feel dumb and unlikable*, notice that this is actually a thought and rewrite it as such: *I think I am dumb and unlikable.*

Step 2: Continue rewriting all the statements that confuse feelings and thoughts. *I feel dumb*, for instance, would be replaced by *I do not think I am as knowledgable as I would like to be, so I will make an effort to learn new things and read more.* Similarly, *I feel unlikable* can be clarified with *I feel lonely, as I have trouble connecting with others. I want to work on connecting with people who have things in common with me.*

Step 3: Notice how feelings based on healthier thoughts transform sadness, hopelessness, and loneliness to hopefulness, confidence, and optimism. Make a habit of doing this exercise regularly so you can catch your negative thoughts that you lump with your feelings and work toward separating them to see a situation more clearly. You can't change feelings directly, but you *can* change thoughts. And you can learn to be more solution-focused instead of problem-focused.

Periodically review your list separating thoughts and feelings, adding to it when new thoughts and feelings come up. Train yourself to be a pro at separating your thoughts from your feelings as you transform problems into solutions.

12: Take Control of Your Thoughts

"Change the way you look at things and the things you look at change."

—Wayne Dyer

People do not make us feel or think a certain way. When we blame our child for driving us crazy, a friend for making us mad, a coworker for making us upset, or bad weather for putting us in a bad mood, we make the mistake of assigning our thoughts and feelings to others rather than taking responsibility for ourselves. The truth is that our feelings cannot change by changing other people or external circumstances. Who is the only person you can change? You got it—yourself!

When we feel upset, depressed, or anxious, all too often we look for reasons outside of ourselves as to why we *feel* a certain way instead of focusing on how we *think* about what happens to us. In actuality, short of physical harm, no one or no situation has the power to make us feel anything. It is really our *perceptions* and *thoughts* about what happens that determine how we feel. To quote pastor and educator Charles Swindoll, "I am convinced that life is 10 percent what happens to me and 90 percent how I react to it."

To underscore this point, here is a sampling of some comments my therapy clients have expressed to me:

"She makes me so mad!"

"This weather is bumming me out."

"He makes me feel bad about myself."

"My teenager is driving me crazy!"

"My boss makes me nervous."

What do you notice about these statements? They all have one thing in common: they all blame personal feelings on events and people rather than on how we *think* about what is happening to us. Once you really believe that you're the only person you can change, you can reframe your thoughts into positive statements that are also more actionable. For example, *She makes me so mad!* can be rephrased as *I am mad when she criticizes me, and I am going to tell her that I will no longer visit if she continues to treat me rudely.*

Notice how a statement showing powerlessness can be turned into one that is empowering not only because it is factual, but also because it offers an actionable takeaway of what we can do to shift our focus from problems to solutions.

Are you ready to change your thoughts to change your moods and take control of your life?

GIVE IT A TRY

Let's first take a look at how a single negative thought can be very powerful.

Step 1: Fill a clear glass with water and put one drop of food coloring in it. Stir it around. Notice how quickly the water changes, even with just a single drop of coloring. Imagine that this drop represents a negative thought, such as *I'm fat* or *I'll never get over this*. As the water discolors, you can see how much power this drop has to color your water—just like a negative thought colors your world!

Step 2: Now add several drops of different colors to the glass, representing many negative thoughts. The water turns muddy, just like the hundreds of negative thoughts that permeate our mind every day, causing us to feel gloomy and dark.

Step 3: After you have filled your glass of water with five to ten drops representing your negative thoughts about yourself or others, get another fresh glass of water. This time add drops of clear water to represent healthier and more positive self-statements to challenge your irrational thoughts. Replace *I'm fat* with *I am fifteen pounds overweight, and I will develop strategies to lose the weight*. Replace *I'll never get over this* with *I will seek out a lot of support to help me get through this*. The water is no longer muddy—it's clear, just like your healthier thoughts that allow you to see things more clearly and accurately. Notice that these examples of rephrasing include actionable solutions to each problem.

Imagine what your life would be like if you took more control of your thoughts and changed negativity to positivity! With these steps, are you ready to challenge your negative thinking?

13: Identify Cognitive Distortions

"The primary cause of unhappiness is never the situation, but your thoughts about it. Be aware of the thoughts you are thinking."

—Eckhart Tolle

"I am fat and unattractive."

"I am a bad mother."

"I will never get over this!"

"It's awful that she said that to me!"

"They think I'm stupid."

"He's just trying to show me up!"

"I know I shouldn't be so upset about it."

What's the common denominator in all these statements? Do you notice that although these statements are stated as absolute facts, they are really just interpretations? Do you notice that all these statements are extreme and blown out of proportion? Do you notice how negatively biased they are instead of being factual and descriptive?

If we cannot identify our destructive thinking habits, we will keep on upsetting ourselves with distorted thinking, which affects all aspects of our lives. Those negative thoughts may lead to negative emotions, poor life adjustment, addictions, social isolation, and toxic relationships.

In chapter 2 the concept of cognitive distortions was introduced in order to understand how to eliminate perfectionistic thinking. Since this concept is so crucial to identifying and eliminating common errors in thinking, we will now explore more about them and how to change them. In addition to the eight types of cognitive distortions defined in chapter 2 (see tip #9), here are a few more categories of distortion that act as barriers to healthy thinking:

- **All-or-Nothing Thinking:** seeing the world in extremes, in terms of "all this" or "all that," with no other in-between possibilities; example: *She hates me!*

- **Blaming:** taking on too much responsibility for things outside of our control; example: *It's all my fault that my child is depressed.*

- **Magnification or Minimization:** exaggerating the import of common occurrences or, on the flip side, downplaying them too much to shield our vulnerability; examples: *It's terrible that she is mad at me* and *It's no big deal.*

- **Mental Filtering:** focusing on the negative aspects of a situation by filtering out the positives; example: *My ears are too big and make me look unattractive.*

- **Mind Reading:** making faulty assumptions about the thoughts, actions, or motivations of others; example: *She's trying to make me look stupid in our weekly meetings.*

Do you notice any self-limiting distortions that you tend to use? Don't you want to think in ways that will help you rather than hurt you?

GIVE IT A TRY

Identifying cognitive distortions helps us develop the objectivity to replace our distorted self-statements with more accurate assessments. This activity is adapted from the "triple column technique" of CBT therapist David Burns (2008).

Step 1: On a blank piece of paper or computer document, create three columns.

Step 2: Title the first column **Automatic Negative Thought,** then populate that column with an example of a troubling thought, such as: *I am fat and not as attractive as any of my friends. I'll never get it together!*

Step 3: Title the second column **Type of Cognitive Error,** then list underneath the type of cognitive distortion(s) this upsetting thought demonstrates. Applicable in this case are *All-or-Nothing Thinking, Magnification, Emotional Reasoning,* and *Labeling.*

Step 4: Title the third column **Rational Alternative Thought.** Once you've noted the type of thinking errors that apply, it is easier to change the thought to a healthier option here. A more factual statement, which is not only free of cognitive distortions but is also an actionable step, would be *I would like to lose twenty pounds to feel better about my body, and it would make me feel more attractive.*

Step 5: With examples from your own life, observe how identifying the types of distortions and creating healthier alternatives will help you be more objective about your distorted thinking and develop more actionable alternatives.

By using the triple column technique, you are well on your way to changing your thoughts to change your life! Aren't you tired of having cognitive distortions fog your ability to see yourself and your life with clear vision?

14: Uncover Your Core Irrational Beliefs

"Change your thoughts and you change your world."

—Norman Vincent Peale

People who do not feel good about themselves tend to interpret what happens to them in life in a self-deprecating and negative way. They tend to blame themselves when things go wrong and have little trouble finding evidence of how they screwed up or how they are not as good as others. They often live in fear of not getting approval from others, but paradoxically, they shy away from others and isolate themselves in fear of being hurt, rejected, or saying something wrong. It is as if they are looking at the world with tinted glasses—or glasses with the wrong prescription!

Do you tend to be self-critical, to be anxious about how others see you, and to interpret situations in a self-doubting way? If so, you will not be able to stop this pattern until you get to the bottom of what your core beliefs are that trigger your anxiety and negative perceptions. Until you uncover your *core irrational beliefs*, you will continue to be negatively triggered by people and events in your world.

Uncovering your core beliefs requires digging deeper into your thoughts. David Burns's "vertical arrow technique" (1989) is very helpful in uncovering the core beliefs at the root of our problematic thoughts and feelings. This technique follows each thought with simple questions like *"Why is this important?"* and *"If this were true, what is causing me to be upset?"* This questioning will help you dig down to your core beliefs.

It works like this:

"I hope they like me."

Q: *"Why is this important? What would it mean to me?"*

"It would be terrible if they did not like me."

Q: *"If this were true, what is causing me to be upset? What would it mean to me?"*

"I need them to approve of me since they are better than me."

Q: *"If this were true, what is causing me to be upset? What would it mean to me?"*

"It would mean I am inferior to others"

Q: *"If this were true, what is causing me to be upset? What would it mean to me?"*

"It would mean I am a failure."

You can see with this model how core irrational beliefs exaggerate the importance of approval from others. With each question, you go deeper and deeper into the core belief that you need to be liked in order to like yourself. Thus, if you keep focusing on wanting to be liked, without digging deeper to the core, you will be focusing your attention on the surface rather than on the real source of your feeling.

Don't you deserve to love yourself—really, really love yourself—despite what others think?

GIVE IT A TRY

Are you ready to dig deep to the core using the vertical arrow technique?

Step 1: Following the model above, identify a thought that is causing you distress. Can you then dig deeper? It might help to visualize a shovel, and with each question, imagine that you are digging deeper toward the root of the problem. Apply the same questions as above: *"Why is that so important to me? What would it mean to me if this were true?"*

Step 2: Keep asking these questions until you get to the bottom of your distressing thought and are able to uncover your core irrational belief. Do you see yourself as helpless, unlovable, or unworthy?

Step 3: After you dig deep to the core, ask yourself these questions:

- *How does the way I see myself reflect the way I see the world?*

- *Does my core belief lead me to see the world as intimidating and other people as judgmental?*

- *Do I have core irrational beliefs that taint my perceptions in my daily interactions?*

- *What do these beliefs say about my assumptions about my life and future?*

Step 4: Now replace the negative, irrational belief you identified with a more rational, factual thought. For example, replace *I'm a failure* with *Making mistakes or even failing at some things does not mean I am a failure. After all, the most successful people fail at times.* How does that change your core belief about yourself?

Remember that feeling good about yourself comes from within by digging deeper—it is not found in the opinions of others. Your worthiness does not have to be earned—you are worthy unconditionally!

15: Eliminate Automatic Negative Thoughts

"Consider that not only do negative thoughts and emotions destroy our experience of peace, they also undermine our health."

—Dalai Lama

The tough part about eliminating negative thoughts is that we often don't even realize we have them. We're just so used to our regular feelings and reactions that we bypass awareness of how our thoughts are actually causing us to feel and react.

Sometimes it's hard to identify our habitual thoughts. To help us out, David Burns (2008) popularized the concept of ANTS, a catchy abbreviation for "automatic negative thoughts," called this because they are almost second nature to us. They reflect our erroneous ways of thinking that distort our perceptions of our world. With distorted ways of looking at ourselves and everything around us, we can easily become anxious, depressed, and overstressed.

With the help of the ANTS visualization, however, we can uncover our unhealthy, largely unconscious thoughts and become more mindful of how we think in unhealthy ways. Recognizing and eradicating these automatic negative thoughts will put you on the right track for recovery, healing, and embracing your greatness.

Are you ready to get rid of those pesky ANTS in your head once and for all?

GIVE IT A TRY

Let's identify your ANTS so you can stop sabotaging your happiness.

Step 1: Start by creating a six-column table that you name **ANTS Diary** either on a piece of paper or on your computer. Then title each column, left to right, in this order:

- *What Are My ANTS?*

- *Percentage of Certainty The ANTS Are True*

- *What Is the Evidence Supporting These Thoughts?*

- *What Is the Evidence Against These Thoughts?*

- *Reframe the Thoughts*

- *Percentage of Certainty the Reframed Thoughts Are True*

You'll notice that both the second and sixth columns ask you for the percentage of certainty you feel about both your ANTS and your healthier replacement thoughts for them. Research has shown that assessing the degree of certainty is helpful in challenging unhealthy thoughts and also in having more confidence in healthier ones (Burns 2008). It also helps to eliminate all-or-nothing thinking when you consider your degree of certainty about the truth of a negative thought.

Step 2: Now it's time to fill in your chart. Here's a sample to get you started:

- For column 1: *She made me furious when she acted so rude.*

- For column 2: 80%

- For column 3: *She was not nice to me.*

- For column 4: *She does not have the power to make me feel anything—I can choose how hurt or not hurt I am.*

- For column 5: *I was upset when she acted rude to me, and even the idea that she was rude was my perception. She did not make me feel anything.*

- For column 6: *100%*

Your ANTS might include thoughts like *I'm no good, I'll never find someone to love,* and *There's something wrong with me.*

Step 3: Examine the evidence of your ANTS to cast some suspicion about their truth. Ask yourself, *What makes them true? Where is the evidence? What are the facts that support my ANTS? Are my self-sabotaging statements factual or merely my faulty perceptions?* Make sure you also rate the degree of certainty you have about your examination of the evidence. Do you have 100 percent confidence in them? 90 percent? 80 percent?

Step 4: Name your ANTS. You can call one Creepy, for example, and each time you note that automatic negative thought popping up in your head, say to yourself, *"There goes the Creep again!"* By naming your ANTS, you distance yourself from them and from believing them.

Step 5: Count your ANTS. By keeping a tally in your diary of how often each of your automatic negative thoughts crawl into your mind, you will develop an awareness of the extent to which these thoughts control your thinking.

How many ANTS were you able to identify? How did you do with naming and examining the evidence? How many ANTS did you name? How many ANTS did you count in a given period? Remember to keep up with tackling your ANT problem in your diary chart to exterminate it once and for all. Stick with it and strive to make your head ANT-free!

4

Embrace Your Past

LEARNING FROM IT INSTEAD OF LIVING IN IT

D o you find that you have trouble coping with your day-to-day life without being pulled down by thoughts about the past? Do you feel like the past is an anchor, weighing you down from enjoying life fully today? If you are like most people plagued with self-doubt and low self-esteem, the answer to these questions is likely yes. But one thing's for sure—the past never changes. The past leaves us with two choices: learn from it or live in it.

Low self-esteem breeds thoughts that get stuck on repeat in your head about the regrettable choices, mistakes, or failures you think you've made. If you keep pondering, churning, and regurgitating the same old stuff, you are demonstrating the digestive process of a cow chewing its cud. The cow actually does digest food by regurgitating the same food over and over again in the *physiological* process called *rumination*. This is the origin of the word for the *psychological* process of rumination—reviewing past mistakes, obsessive thoughts, missed opportunities, regrettable actions and choices…regurgitating the same stuff over and over and over again.

If you find that you spend too much time looking back on your choices and actions—reviewing what was, what could have been, or what should have been—then you will never be able to fully live today. After all, what's done is done—*over*. There's a long list of things we can repeatedly mull over. The only hope to move forward is to focus more on what's left rather than on what we lost or left behind. This transitions us from post-traumatic stress to post-traumatic growth.

Are you ready to stop giving your past more power than your present? Don't you deserve to free yourself from the chains of your past and allow yourself to experience your life fully *now?*

16: Forgive the Past

"Forgiveness is giving up the hope of a better past."
—Lily Tomlin

In life there are no shortages of injustices to collect. There are no shortages of opportunities to feel like you've been wronged, taken advantage of, overlooked, treated poorly, and subject to careless treatment. Despite the many variations of wrongs that we can be subject to—backbiting at the office, being the unsuspecting casualty of a family feud, mistreatment by a friend or lover, rude put-downs by others, emotional distancing or betrayal by your spouse or someone close to you—the question inevitably remains: *"Now what?"*

Some people never get there—they never get to *"Now what?"* or *"What's next?"* because they are still too stuck in *"Why?"* They spin their wheels reworking yesterday and what should have happened, getting stuck in the land of "woulda, coulda, shoulda." I have found all too many clients tending to choose self-righteous indignation over acceptance, and grudges over forgiveness, digging themselves even deeper into the unfairness of it all. Unfortunately, this negativity only serves to fast-track them for a life of anger and discontent.

It is a common misperception that forgiveness is all about the other person, because it is really about yourself. It is about you having the conviction to refuse to be defined by past hurts.

Forgiveness is ultimately about moving on from the victim role and refusing to be defined by bitterness rather than condoning the actions of others.

How about you? Are you ready to stop being a collector of injustices and move ahead, albeit bruised but wiser?

GIVE IT A TRY

A large part of the work of forgiveness involves changing your own personal story—not the reality, just your interpretation of it.

Step 1: If you feel like you are held back in life by grievances, grudges, and anger, start by writing down your story. Write how you've felt unfairly treated by people or by life. Here are some questions to help you reflect:

- *How were you hurt?*

- *How has it affected you even today?*

- *How does it hold you back from enjoying life, trusting others, and opening yourself up to new experiences?*

- *How do you think things should have gone?*

- *How would your life be different if some of these things never happened or merely happened differently?*

- *What about the past makes it just too hard to "get over"?*

Step 2: Analyze what you've written:

- *What do you notice? Do you see yourself more as a victim in life than a victor?*

- *Are you too focused on how right you were and how you did not get a fair shake?*

- *Are you waiting for others to make amends—to apologize or be different—for you to reach some peace?*

- *Do you realize you can forgive them even if they're not sorry—and just not go back for more?*

Step 3: As you look over your answers, reflect on what is keeping you stuck in bitterness, making you a victim of the past. Then, considering your answers to all of the questions above, rewrite your story to make yourself less like a victim of your past and more open to forgiveness and healing. For example, if you wrote, *They were such jerks*, rewrite a new version of that statement: *People sure can be hurtful.*

Step 4: Look at your rewritten story and ask yourself if it is in the voice of a victim or the voice of a victorious survivor. If you find that your story is still steeped in bitterness, fine-tune it again to reflect resiliency and courage.

Isn't it time to change your story? Remember, forgiveness is about *your* healing—it is not about who is right or what is fair. It is just about you not being a hostage to the past anymore.

17: Overcome Regret

"Never look back unless you are planning to go that way."
—Henry David Thoreau

There's nothing like the sharp sting of regret to keep you stuck in the past and mess up your life. Regret is a tough nut to crack and is definitely a self-esteem robber. It is only human to have regrets, and in hindsight almost all of us would have made some different choices "back then." Regrets can irritate you like grains of sand in your shoe. They form a collective, persistent voice that adds fuel to the fire that destroys self-esteem—beating you up and keeping you down. Your regrets can be a great teacher to help you improve yourself and your choices moving forward, but if you have low self-esteem, you will be less likely to use regrets as motivating rather than debilitating. Regrets not only deplete us of self-esteem, but they also give rise to anxiety and depression. Regrets keep us stuck in the past, causing us to endlessly rework old issues that can never be changed. They lurk in the recesses of our mind, like a slow poison leaking into every day of our lives.

Psychologist Neal Roese (2005) offers four general common areas of regret:

1. Regrets about educational choices

2. Regrets about career choices

3. Regrets about love

4. Regrets about parenting

Roese emphasizes that regrets are not all bad—in fact, they can be quite productive if you focus on lessons learned and new actions built on a foundation of regrets. He makes the distinction between *productive* and *unproductive* regrets. He urges us to use regrets as a springboard to take different action now, building on regrets rather than being crippled by them. In essence, we can use regret to remind us that we can do better instead of scold us that we should have done better.

How about you? Are you plagued by regrets that interfere with you living in the now? Are you ready to take control of your regrets today and embrace them to move past them?

GIVE IT A TRY

How would life be different for you if you were able to truly embrace your flawed, imperfect self? Learning strategies to build on your regrets rather than get buried under them will help you move forward to embrace your greatness.

Step 1: Following Roese's lead, let's turn unproductive regrets into productive regrets. Label two columns on a blank sheet as shown on the next page. In the first column list the regrets that keep plaguing you. In the second, write down some ideas on how to make those regrets productive based on committing yourself to actions *now*.

Unproductive Regret	Productive Regret
I chose the wrong career.	I can explore new alternatives and choices now, like going back to school or getting more training.
I screwed up my marriage.	I am learning valuable lessons about how to control my anger and treat others more assertively. I'm already a much more nurturing and calmer parent and friend, and I will be healthier in my relationships going forward.
I burned many bridges with people close to me.	I will be careful to be kind to those close to me now, accept responsibility for hurting them, and act better now.

Step 2: To further work on overcoming unproductive regrets, reflect on these questions and write out your answers:

- *Can you forgive yourself for not having the foresight to know what is now so obvious in hindsight? Why or why not?*

- *How can your life change if you commit to focusing on being motivated by your regrets rather than being defined and debilitated by them?*

- *What have you learned from the lessons your regret has taught you?*

Step 3: Be patient with yourself as you work through your regrets, and revisit this activity regularly. Continually refine your tangible goals to make them specific calls to action. As you work to let go of your regrets, remember to never give your past more power than your present.

What is your plan to turn your unproductive regrets into more productive ones? Isn't it about time to give yourself another shot and leave your regrets behind?

18: Move from "Why?" to "What's Next?"

"Do not say, 'Why were the old days better than these?' For it is not wise to ask such questions."

—Ecclesiastes

When I ask new clients what they want to get out of therapy, I am often struck by how many of them answer that they want help to figure out "why" something has happened. It's as if they think that is the magic bullet that will make them well; but in reality, it's only part of the answer, because it focuses on the past and not on solutions.

There are endless "why" questions we could pose:

"Why is he so shy?"

"Why didn't she listen to me?"

"Why did that happen to me?"

"Why was I so foolish?"

"Why can't I get my life together?"

"WHY, WHY, WHY?"

Imagine for a moment being a passenger in a car when the driver, your friend, ran a stop sign, resulting in an accident in which you broke a leg. Regardless of why the driver was so care-less, why he was not paying attention, or why he didn't look the other way, the fact remains that your leg is broken. Maybe you suspect he was drinking—you really don't know.

Aside from not driving with him again, what can you do about it? In essence, asking *"Why?"* keeps you stuck in the past, whereas *"What's next?"* is about taking action now and planning for your future. Concentrating on what comes next is the mind-set we need to build on lessons learned and move forward. The windows of opportunity to change the reasons why are closed. Look back long enough to learn from it, then it's time to move on. Basically, it's not wise to ask too many whys!

This is where SMART goals come in. SMART is a mne-monic acronym originated by businessman George Doran (1981) that variably stands for: specific, measurable, action-oriented, realistic, and time-bound.

Are you ready to turn your "whys" into SMART goals? Wouldn't it be nice to have a specific action plan to move forward?

GIVE IT A TRY

SMART goals will help you make tangible changes as you move from past regret to living with a present focus.

Step 1: Write down at least three examples of "why" questions that keep you stuck in the past.

Step 2: For each question you wrote, follow it with an idea of how to move on from "*Why?*" and look to "*What's next?*" by using this model to differentiate between the two thought patterns:

Why?	What's Next?
Why am I so undisciplined with exercise?	*I will create a fitness and exercise plan I can stick to.*
Why does he act so rude to me?	*When he's rude, I will let him know I will not respond until he addresses me more respectfully.*
Why don't people like me?	*I will work on liking myself first instead of worrying about others by doing self-help reading and exercises.*

Step 3: After shifting your focus to present-focused goals, apply the SMART model to them to make them more achievable. For example, for the first goal above:

- **Specific:** *I will commit myself to walking regularly to get back into shape. I will look for various ways to walk off the pounds.*

- **Measurable:** *I plan to walk 10,000 steps a day, four days per week.*

- **Action-Oriented:** *I will use the treadmill for half an hour each day. I will also park my car at the far end of the parking* *lot to build more exercise into my everyday life. For variety, I will alternate the treadmill with walking outside or at the mall on weekends, when I have more time.*

- **Realistic:** *This plan fits well into my lifestyle and my working hours. I will schedule the 10,000 steps for the two days I leave work early and for Saturday and Sunday.*

- **Time-Bound:** *I will follow this plan for three weeks; at the end of that span I will reevaluate to decide if I will continue on this plan or modify it.*

Are you ready to get SMART with your goals? After all, how are you going to be able to embrace your greatness if you focus on the "whys" of the past instead of on constructive actions for the present and future?

19: Grow Past the Past with Acceptance

"My happiness grows in direct proportion to my acceptance, and in inverse proportion to my expectations."

—Michael J. Fox

Sometimes the past is just hard to accept—either that it is over or that it never was all that it was cracked up to be and that there are no second chances. Sometimes so much of our identity is caught up in the past that we see moving on as letting go of too much of ourselves.

Whether you've had trauma in the past, feel like you peaked in junior high and never quite "made it" after that, miss a loved one you can't get back, or see your life as "all downhill from here," you can always find a reason to look back wistfully with longing, regret, and a sense of loss.

I have been struck with how getting over the past and reaching some sense of acceptance is much like the grieving process. Swiss psychiatrist Elisabeth Kübler-Ross (1969) developed the concept of the five stages of grieving that people go through as they face their own impending death. This model has also been widely applied to the stages people go through as they mourn the impending or actual loss of a loved one. The final stage to move toward is that of acceptance.

This model can offer us help in coping with many common life losses: our health, our youth, our dreams, our dashed hopes, and relationships that have ended. Sometimes the grieving process entails mourning the loss of what never actually even happened, despite wanting it so badly. If you don't reach the state of acceptance, you might find yourself spending a lot of time reviewing missed opportunities and disappointments and staying angry that your dreams were thwarted or just never came true.

Here is a sample of the thought patterns associated with each of the five stages of grieving. No matter how big or small your losses might seem, the process is the same. The progression does not always follow a straight path—sometimes we go back and forth between stages, revisiting a stage after we think we are "over it," so it is important to be patient with yourself as you go along the healing journey to acceptance and growth from the hurt.

Stage 1: *Denial*

Grieving Death: *I avoid facing the likelihood of my death.*

I cannot face mortality, and I feel like I am invincible.

Grieving from Hurtful Memories: *I don't admit I am or ever was hurt.*

I see things like I want to see them, not as they are.

Stage 2: *Anger*

Grieving Death: *I am angry at life's unfairness.*

I am filled with resentment and can't forgive.

Grieving from Hurtful Memories: *I blame others for hurting me.*

Others are responsible for my pain. I can't forgive. Anger consumes me.

Stage 3: *Bargaining*

Grieving Death: *I set up conditions to be fulfilled before I die.*

If I act or think certain ways, I can change outcomes.

Grieving from Hurtful Memories: *I set up conditions to be met before I'm ready to forgive.*

If I act in a certain way, perhaps I can get others to change their mind or behaviors.

Stage 4: *Depression*

Grieving Death: *I blame myself for not fulfilling my dreams.*

I have much regret.

Grieving from Hurtful Memories: *I blame myself for my loss.*

Regrets consume me, and I cannot live fully in the present. I feel hopeless.

Stage 5: *Acceptance*

Grieving Death: *I have prepared for my death and made requests of how my affairs should be handled.*

I have come to terms with my mortality and my legacy.

Grieving from Hurtful Memories: *I look forward to growth from hurt. My bitterness is gradually being replaced by a sense of gratefulness.*

I have accepted my limitations and will build on my life lessons.

Whether you feel a sense of loss over something that happened or something that never did, don't you deserve to heal?

GIVE IT A TRY

The model for the five stages of grief can help you heal from past resentments and trauma.

Step 1: Think of a loss you have had that has had a profound impact on you. It can be either a concrete loss or a psychological loss—they follow the same progression. Looking at the sample model above, ask yourself how it relates to you. What do you need to reach the stage of acceptance?

Step 2: Chart your own grieving process by writing down each stage of grief, accompanied by your thought(s) there. Remember as you do this that mourning is not necessarily a linear process. As we grieve, we can keep going back and forth from one stage to another (sometimes depending on what triggers us in everyday life) as we move toward the final goal of reaching acceptance.

Step 3: For the example you chose, look at where you are in the process of grieving and healing. Reflect on these questions:

- *What stops you from reaching the last stage of acceptance?*

- *Can you identify what you need to help you move through the stages instead of getting stuck?*

- *What do you need to do to make peace and build on your lessons learned?*

Step 4: Consider sharing this assignment with someone you trust. Part of healing is asking for support and encouragement from others. Just the process of opening up and expressing your thoughts to someone who can give you support will be a key to get you through. If you don't trust that you have a person like that in your life, seeking professional counseling can prove life-changing.

With the help of this model, do you have a plan to move past grief to growth? If you find yourself focusing on wasted time lost forever, isn't it time to shift your focus to what you can gain moving forward?

20: Embrace Post-Traumatic Growth

> *"'Finding the path up' is what separates the successful from those who give up. It requires that you look for the opportunity in any setback, rather than settling in to despair."*

—Shawn Achor

Trauma happens in a variety of ways. Many types of events can cause a setback that is hard to move past. Some examples of unrelenting trauma include going through a difficult breakup, becoming estranged from a loved one, getting a life-threatening diagnosis, suffering a huge financial setback, losing a job or business, failing at a life dream, being the survivor of a war or a natural disaster, experiencing physical assault or a tragic accident (involving you or a loved one), and grieving the death of someone close to you.

Author and lecturer Shawn Achor writes about post-traumatic growth in his book *The Happiness Advantage* (2010). He uses the term "falling up" instead of "falling down" to describe the process of recovering from a stressful event and changing for the better because of the trauma. He believes that great suffering paves the way to the greatest changes. When you fall up, you are never really the same—you are actually better because of the growth you experience from your recovery. Positive psychological growth can be seen in survivors of trauma who dedicate their energies to creating something bigger than themselves to help others who face a similar setback. Achor himself attributes his own period of depression as a graduate student with helping him understand how to overcome adversity and stress to change his mind-set, enabling him to be more compassionate, understanding, and able to help people though his life's work on happiness.

How about you? Are you ready to get a new lease on life by moving past your past with a growth mind-set and a focus on resilience?

GIVE IT A TRY

Using Shawn Achor's idea of "falling up," you can transform post-traumatic stress into post-traumatic growth.

Step 1: Write down the three greatest moments of personal growth in your life. Describe how you have grown from these three moments, aided by these prompts:

- *Did the greatest times of growth result from adversity?*

- *What lessons did you learn?*

- *How have they helped you be a better person?*

- *Have you developed more empathy for others?*

- *Have these experiences made you wiser and more insightful?*

Step 2: Write down some concrete actions you can take to empower yourself to face the challenges in front of you now. For example, if you are suffering a health scare, think of concrete ways that you can take control of your health.

Step 3: Tell someone you can confide in about your plan of action. Research has shown that seeking social support and having a strong social network are the best predictors of growth after setbacks.

Step 4: Write out a list of at least three ways to build your support system and community of caring. Building a close network can take many forms, including reaching out to friends, making an effort to make new ones, joining a new club or activity, and opening up to others you trust.

If you find yourself suffering from post-traumatic stress, have you made a plan to shift to post-traumatic growth as you seek support, open yourself to asking for help, and widen your circle of caring?

Embrace
Self~Compassion

LEARNING TO BE KIND
TO YOURSELF

Who wouldn't feel good acing a test, receiving a promotion, scoring a winning point, or getting a compliment? Feeling good about your accomplishments and striving to be competent and successful is healthy. Most of us certainly strive to do our best and take pride in a job well done. The problem comes when you equate your self-worth with your stellar performance or the approval of others.

Current research has been less focused on the traditional concept of self-esteem, which is *conditional*, based on earning it. Instead, loving ourselves even when we fail embodies true self-esteem, which is why *self-compassion* offers an alternative to the conditional notion of esteem. Researcher Brené Brown (2010) is a big proponent of this new view of self-esteem, focusing on how to truly love yourself by overcoming shame and perfectionism, embracing vulnerability, and living wholeheartedly. Her "Power of Vulnerability" presentation is one of the most widely watched TED Talks, with more than 31 million views.

Brown's work is complemented by another researcher, Kristin Neff (2011), who is a leading authority on self-compassion. Neff regards the traditional notion of self-esteem as overly focused on being better than average, while self-compassion is all about accepting yourself unconditionally without comparisons. That holds even when you make a big mistake and experience failure.

This newer concept of self-esteem shifts the spotlight away from one's performance, success, and comparisons with others and onto unconditional self-acceptance and self-compassion.

Good thing too—if self-esteem really were rooted in being "above average," half the population would consequently be in the lower 50 percent and thus regarded as inadequate and unsuccessful. But this newer perspective on self-esteem is liberating because regardless of whether you are earning a C grade in a class or got accepted to your dream school, you can still feel just as happy and good about yourself.

This chapter's tips will explore ways to turn traditional self-esteem into self-compassion, reduce shame-based thinking, and achieve the level of happiness that you want and deserve. Self-compassion will allow you to embrace your vulnerability and to live wholeheartedly, without fear of disapproval, rejection, or failure.

Are you ready to give up your notions of who you "should be" and embrace who you really are?

21: Say Hello to Self-Compassion

"Insecurity, anxiety, and depression are incredibly common in our society, and much of this is due to self-judgment, to beating ourselves up when we feel we aren't winning the game of life."

—Kristin Neff

By now you know that self-esteem is important for a happy life. The question comes down to *how you get it*. How do you get yours? As we aim to transition from conditional self-esteem to unconditional self-love, let's look at what you're basing your self-esteem on:

- *Do you get those good feelings about yourself from your achievements and the approval of others?*

- *Do you have to do anything to deserve good feelings about yourself, or are you worthy without needing proof?*

- *Do you get your basic sense of self-worth by coming out ahead when you compare yourself with others?*

- *Do you think you need to make a lot of money, have a prestigious job, or own an impressive home or a high-end car to feel good about yourself?*

- *Do you find yourself comparing yourself to others too much, feeling inferior next to them?*

If you answer yes to even one of these questions, your self-esteem is on shaky ground. Conditional self-esteem based on performance and the evaluation of others is very tenuous. Unconditional self-esteem based on self-compassion and self-acceptance is unshakable.

When your love for and acceptance of yourself is based on comparing yourself to others, the approval of others, and your achievements, the targets for feeling good about yourself will always be changing. There's always someone bound to be better at something than you are, or smarter, more attractive, luckier, richer. There'll always be someone who has more impressive kids, better friends, a more accomplished résumé. Some people have qualities that you might lack altogether.

Does redefining self-esteem mean that it does not matter what we do or how we perform? Of course not! It's great to be challenged and motivated to do your best. Healthy people want to do well and strive to do their best. We just need to eliminate the unhealthy notion that you are only worthy when you excel or hit the mark. If your self-esteem is based on self-compassion, you can win or lose and love yourself anyway.

Are you ready to love yourself unconditionally no matter what? If not, what's getting in the way?

GIVE IT A TRY

There are ways to develop good feelings about yourself that are healthy and unshakable, instead of built on a list of your successes and judgments in comparison to others.

Step 1: Write down at least ten things that make you feel like you are a worthy person.

Step 2: Ask yourself which items fit into the traditional concept of conditional self-esteem and which items are based on nonjudgmental self-compassion.

Step 3: To help you further differentiate unshakable from the shakable self-esteem, put SC next to the answers that show self-compassion and SE next to those that reflect self-esteem based on achievement. For example, if one of your list items is *I get good grades in school*, you would mark that statement with *SE* since your feelings of worthiness are based on performance. There is nothing wrong with being proud of doing well, it just should not be a condition for loving yourself. An example of a self-compassionate statement would be *I am trustworthy, ethical, and caring.* This is not evaluative—it's about who you *are*, not what you *do*.

Step 4: Look at the items you labeled *SE* and change them into more self-compassionate statements. For instance, *I am a top performer at work* could be changed to: *I am proud of my work ethic and enjoy my job. I have developed a great deal of knowledge and expertise that has helped me contribute to the company.*

Take these steps to develop unshakable self-esteem. How does it feel to say good-bye to self-judgment and hello to self-compassion?

22: Forgive Yourself, for Goodness' Sake!

"I did then what I knew how to do. Now that I know better, I do better."

—Maya Angelou

Okay, you've made mistakes. You've goofed. How long are you going to beat yourself up for your less-than-stellar moments? Whether you lost your cool, chose the wrong job, picked the wrong college or regret never having gone at all, drank too much, pushed a loved one away, realized only too late what you had, did poorly at a presentation or flunked a test, life goes on.

The important questions are:

- *Did you learn from your regrets and past actions and choices?*

- *Are you using those choices and even errors in judgment as springboards to having more insight and maturity now?*

- *Are you currently making decisions that you are happy with based on the wisdom you earned?*

Self-forgiveness is the first step in freeing yourself from self-judgment. If your inner critic keeps reminding you how you screwed up, you'll spend too much of your life beating yourself up instead of building yourself up. Without being kind and forgiving to yourself, you will always be at war with yourself. Reworking things that you said or might have said over and over won't help you or anyone else, it'll just keep you emotionally beaten up and bruised.

So are you ready to accept yourself no matter how much you screwed up? Don't you deserve to have some peace?

GIVE IT A TRY

The following exercise can help you look at yourself as you would a friend.

Step 1: Think of a time when you messed up and were especially hard on yourself for it. How would you view the same issue differently if someone else made the same mistake? If you are like most people, you have much more compassion for the imperfections of others.

Step 2: Turn your attention to someone you admire. If that person acted the same way you did, how would you see it differently? How much more accepting and kinder would you be?

Step 3: As you consider this person you admire, visualize that person fading away as you take that person's place. What do you see? Sure, this person messed up, but has your perspective shifted from criticism and judgment to compassion and forgiveness? Can you understand the circumstances that led to the mistake?

Next time you find yourself beating yourself up, remember this visualization and try to treat yourself as your own best friend!

23: Put an End to Shame

"Shame is the intensely painful feeling or experience of believing that we are flawed and therefore unworthy of love and belonging."

—Brené Brown

"Shame on you!" "You should be ashamed of yourself!" "Aren't you ashamed?" Unfortunately, these phrases are commonly used tactics that parents and caregivers use to teach children right from wrong and keep them "in line." Well-meaning parents do not realize that this type of shaming can cause children to doubt themselves. In the name of discipline, caregivers often end up planting seeds of unworthiness. The sad thing is that these parents, teachers, and caregivers heard the same thing growing up too!

No one deserves to go through life with a sense of basic unworthiness. Some of us define ourselves by shame, wallowing in it like a blanket that surrounds us. Harboring a sense of shame can be very isolating. When we feel "bad" and "unworthy," we have a hard time letting our guard down and trusting people, partly because we can't even trust ourselves.

It is important to differentiate shame from guilt. Guilt can be healthy to a point, as it helps us learn from our mistakes and take responsibility for them. Guilt lets us correct our behaviors, but shame just makes us feel bad about ourselves. Here is how they differ:

Shame	Guilt
Core sense of worthlessness	Core sense of worthiness
Remorse turns to self-loathing	Remorse leads to growth and change
Feeling flawed	Feeling responsible
Leads to self-destructive behavior	Leads to learning from mistakes
Focused on inherent badness	Focused on regrettable behaviors
Feels unworthy in relationships	Feels worthy of connection
Problems with intimacy	More likely to have intimate relationships
Bad behaviors make us feel bad	Remorse for behaviors spurs healthier actions

The one thing about shame that many of us fail to realize is that the shame we have is not just about us—it affects everyone around us. Our sadness and negativity permeate our relationships, we have less energy for others, and we tend to never let our guard down for fear of being hurt, rejected, or critiqued. We are not so much fun to be around. Ironically, when you beat yourself up, you are hurting those who love you too—you are not the only one who suffers!

How about you? Do you use guilt to motivate, or does shame hold you back and debilitate you?

GIVE IT A TRY

This shame-busting exercise can be an important step toward self-love and self-compassion.

Step 1: If you feel a sense of shame, write down reasons why. Be specific: What is shameful about you? You might reflect on things you have done or ways in which you find yourself unappealing.

Step 2: Now challenge your reasoning. Ask yourself, *Are these rational or irrational thoughts?* A sample irrational thought is: *I am a bad person.* More rational thoughts to challenge that self-critical assessment could be *My fear of disapproval is a sign of my lack of confidence, not that I am bad or unlikable. I need to work on loving myself first so I won't project my dislike of myself onto others.*

Step 3: Can you identify any messages that foster the habit of self-recrimination? Ask yourself, *Have I used shame as a motivator? Am I afraid that if I am not hard on myself, I will "slack off"?*

Actually, the opposite is true. Shame debilitates you, increases anxiety, and makes you less productive.

Step 4: Devise an action plan and new goals to change your toxic thoughts to less shaming ones. For example, *I will practice working on speaking up with people even about little things, so I can get more comfortable expressing myself. I will also do some reading on assertiveness. And I will curb using drinking as a way to escape feelings.* As you can see, an action plan includes not only those behaviors to increase, but the self-damaging behaviors you want to decrease.

Step 5: If you implement the steps above, how would you feel differently about your life, exchanging shame for healthy guilt, learning from your missteps, and devising an action plan to move forward? How would you feel about yourself if you focused on making amends and worked on repairing damage instead of beating yourself up?

Taking these small but significant steps will help you embrace the fact that no matter how you screwed up or how many wrong turns you think you made, no one deserves to live in shame. You are awesome no matter what (and that's from one awesome person to another)!

24: Allow Yourself to Be Vulnerable

"Vulnerability is the birthplace of love, belonging, joy, courage, empathy, and creativity. It is the source of hope, empathy, accountability, and authenticity."

—Brené Brown

Despite the fact that most people think of vulnerability as a weakness, the opposite is true. Vulnerability is something to embrace and necessary to live authentically and wholeheartedly. Although most of us have learned that being vulnerable is a defect, it actually can make us stronger and more genuine. It helps us be open emotionally and flexible to change and growth.

By avoiding showing our vulnerability to others, we ironically end up making ourselves vulnerable to bad choices and sometimes even addictive behaviors. All too many people risk their emotional and physical health by resorting to numbing themselves with alcohol, drugs, food, or other addictions because they won't reach out to others and cannot accept their feelings of vulnerability.

Does this apply to you? Do you spend too much energy "playing it safe"? Do you numb yourself to avoid feeling weak and vulnerable? When you come from a place of fear and anxiety, protecting yourself to avoid feeling vulnerable will actually end up making you more shaky and insecure.

Are you ready to take the plunge and let yourself be more open to asking for and receiving help from others? Are you ready to embrace your vulnerability?

GIVE IT A TRY

You can take steps to experience the strong side of vulnerability, since admitting that you feel weak and being open to help are actually signs of strength.

Step 1: Picture yourself as a helpless infant, completely vulnerable and trusting of others. If you have a picture of yourself as a baby, take it out and look at it. Can you develop compassion for this vulnerable, sweet infant who is full of beauty and hope?

Step 2: Make it a point in your everyday life to observe the beautiful vulnerability of young children and remind yourself that you are just as beautiful. They are not shielding themselves, they seek help, they don't compare their finger-painting skills to the other kids at school, they don't worry that they don't know the alphabet as well as the kid next door. They can ask questions without feeling stupid.

Step 3: On note cards write down some affirmations to remind yourself of your intrinsic worth: *It's a beautiful thing to look to others for support. I am beautiful and worthy. I am precious and deserve a good life.* Keep these cards in a box or jar to read as a daily practice—pick one or two every day. Choose one statement to be your mantra for the day. You might find it helpful to read your affirmations aloud while looking in the mirror.

Allowing yourself to be vulnerable, feel weak, and seek support can ironically become your greatest strength. After all, if you can't embrace your vulnerability, how in the world can you embrace your greatness?

25: Cultivate Loving Self-Kindness

"With self-kindness, we soothe and comfort our troubled minds. We make a peace offering of warmth, gentleness, and sympathy from ourselves to ourselves, so that true healing can occur."

—Kristin Neff

When our self-esteem is low, this is a clear indication that we are too hard on ourselves. Whether you feel like you are not good enough or think that only by being hard on yourself will you avoid being lazy and complacent, the judgments and demands you place on yourself will not result in happiness or inner peace. Although some think that self-criticism is motivating, in reality, it breeds a sense of anxiety, which hinders creativity, productivity, and our relationships with others.

Kristin Neff (2011) outlines three basic solutions to be self-compassionate instead of self-critical:

- **Self-Kindness:** Think of yourself as a friend and a good person. Be gentle, warm, and understanding no matter what you do wrong instead of being self-flagellating, angry, and critical.

- **Common Humanity:** Keep in mind that you are not alone and that struggling is a part of being human. Being human entails some degree of pain, loss, and challenge; rather than feeling isolated by these experiences, take comfort in knowing there are universal issues that all humans need to go through. Suffering and feelings of inadequacy and aloneness are part of a shared human experience.

- **Mindfulness:** This is the practice of being present-focused and receptive to what is around you with non-judgmental awareness. When you are present-centered in awareness, you are no longer a victim of your past or caught in the what-ifs of your future—you are not swept up in distractions that take you away from being *present*. In times of difficulty you can distance yourself from your thoughts and feelings without necessarily reacting to them and upsetting yourself with them.

Are you ready to focus on being kind to yourself, to feel connected to a larger universe through a sense of common humanity, and to change your life today?

GIVE IT A TRY

The three areas of self-compassion can help us quell our inner critic and embrace our greatness.

Step 1: For each of the three components of self-compassion outlined by Neff, write at least one example of how to apply the concept to yourself.

Step 2: Give yourself some physical reassurance, such as a gentle stroke on your arm, a rub of your neck, a hand over the area of your heart. Be mindful of the sensations you feel as you focus on self-compassion. How does it feel to be warm and loving to yourself?

Step 3: How about giving yourself a hug or a kiss? Hershey's Hugs and Kisses can be a visual (and tasty!) reminder of the importance of displays of affection for ourselves. This type of tangible prompt can also remind you to be kind to others and spread the love.

How does it feel to take these simple steps to remind you of your greatness? Isn't it better to treat yourself as a friend instead of an adversary? Don't you deserve that?

Embrace Mindfulness

LEARNING TO BE PRESENT

In this chapter we will explore more deeply the concept of *mindfulness*, which is now a cornerstone to most current psychological theories and treatments. Despite the fact that many people think of mindfulness as almost synonymous with meditation, mindfulness is much more than that. Sitting quietly with eyes closed, breathing deeply in a meditative state, is just one example of mindfulness. Mindfulness, as modern psychological treatments define it, is a practice that doesn't isolate you from the world, but rather makes you more aware of yourself and the world in the present. Simply put, mindfulness is the practice of *nonjudgmental awareness*.

So whether you are sitting in lotus position on a mountaintop, driving in a car during rush hour, eating breakfast, working, sitting in class, playing a video game, watching TV, taking a shower, walking, planting flowers, or doing laundry, mindful awareness will help you experience life in the present without being torn by ruminations from the past or worries about the future.

For a practical example of how mindfulness can help you in everyday life, imagine that you are a student taking a difficult exam. If you find the test harder than you expected, you could find yourself distracted with a variety of negative thoughts. You might beat yourself up for not studying enough, you might be riddled with anxiety about how you will do, you might be mad at the teacher for making the test so unfair, or you might be looking around to get clues on how everyone else is reacting to the test. You might doubt your intelligence and feel overwhelmed as you ask yourself when or if your life will ever fall into place. You might have visceral reactions, such as sweaty palms, racing heart, rapid breathing, or feeling sick to your stomach over all the ruminations and worry. All these examples, which are quite common, are the *opposite* of mindfulness.

How would the same situation look if you were mindful? You might have some of these fleeting thoughts, but instead of identifying with them and paying much attention to them, you'd let these thoughts come and go without getting unnerved by them. Rather than getting too attached to what is going through your mind, you'd be aware of the thoughts without getting upset by them. You'd focus on the task at hand—not paying much mind to the running commentary in your head about how you screwed up—feeling calm instead of agitated. Your physical sensations would be more relaxed and stable.

Which approach sounds more like you? If you are like many people, you can identify more with the first scenario, but you'd love to have the attitude shown in the second scenario. Mindfulness can help us considerably in finding peace and happiness in everyday life.

26: Develop Mindfulness in Everyday Life

"There are only two days in the year that nothing can be done. One is called yesterday and the other is called tomorrow, so today is the right day to love, believe, do, and mostly live."

—Dalai Lama

Mindfulness increases our awareness of everyday life. Mindfulness strategies offer a life practice that helps us live more fully, manage stress, and improve our health emotionally as well as physically through present-centered living. The ability to be mindful helps to manage our negative thoughts and boost our self-love and self-esteem.

As the study of mindfulness grows, we learn more and more how to incorporate a mindfulness mind-set into our daily lives. Despite the variety of practices and techniques, there are certain things that all mindfulness strategies have in common. Here are some of the common elements:

- Nonjudgmental awareness, with which you accept things that cannot be changed

- Mentally noting and observing, viewing things impartially and objectively

- Self-acceptance instead of self-criticism and evaluations of unworthiness

- A present-centered focus that eliminates excessive rumination and worry

- Emphasis on the sensations of all five senses—what you see, feel, taste, hear, and smell

- An attitude of gratitude and acceptance instead of a tendency to judge how things "should be"

- Looking at the world with a fresh perspective, often called a "beginner's mind," with which you have child-like awareness

- Flexible thinking in lieu of biases and stereotypes

These elements of mindfulness help us relax into a happier life as we become more focused on life as it is, being open to what is happening *now*. Self-esteem never thrives when we spend so much time living in our judgmental heads, being haunted by our past or anxious about the future.

Are you ready to work on becoming more mindful? Don't you want to live more peacefully in the moment instead of so much in your head?

GIVE IT A TRY

Assembling a "mindfulness toolbox" is a tangible and practical way to incorporate mindfulness reminders into your life

Step 1: Choose some kind of container—like a shoebox, tote, crate, or basket—that can serve as your mindfulness toolbox. For this toolbox think of things that you find soothing in times of stress. Think of actual objects, pictures, or words you can write on note cards to remind you of affirmations, quotes, or tips to help you stay mindful.

Step 2: After thinking about what will help you stay present-focused, start assembling items that stimulate your five senses. These are some examples:

- **Sense of smell:** a cinnamon stick, mint, scented soaps, incense, scented candle

- **Sense of taste:** chocolate, raisins, apple, granola bar, water or tea

- **Sense of sight:** a picture of loved ones, a snow globe to shake and watch settle (or make your own with glitter and glue), a kaleidoscope, soothing images from magazines or the Internet

- **Sense of touch:** soothing lotion, a soft or furry stuffed animal, a stress ball, Play-Doh

- **Sense of hearing:** a meditation bell, small chimes, Baoding chime balls (Chinese health balls)

Step 3: Now think of ways that you can use the items in your toolbox to help you be more mindful in your everyday life, to limit being distracted by past ruminations and worries about the future. The toolbox will give you some practical ways to stay present-focused.

What are some ideas you have to make up your own mindfulness toolbox? What reminders do you need to help you remain calm in tough times or enhance the good times when you are practicing mindfulness? With your own personalized mindfulness toolbox, you can enjoy the power of living in the moment so you can be comfortable in your own skin, heal from the past, and truly appreciate your life now and embrace your greatness.

27: Practice Mindfulness to Distance from Negative Thoughts

"How people treat you is their karma; how you react is yours."

—Wayne Dyer

Have you ever tried to distance yourself from your upsetting thoughts by watching them like a movie? Do you try to step back and observe your thoughts and feelings before you react to them? Can you pull back from an emotionally charged situation to get a more objective perspective? Do you ever focus on looking *at* your thoughts rather than *from* your thoughts? If so, you are practicing a cornerstone of one of the newest popular therapeutic modalities: acceptance and commitment therapy, developed by Steven Hayes (2005).

Hayes suggests that when you find yourself gripped by toxic thoughts, your unhealthy thoughts are stuck to your mind in a process of *cognitive fusion*. In other words, your cognition—or thought—is *fused* to your way of thinking. Only by distancing from those thoughts by watching them and observing them—that is, by *defusing* from your mind—will your perceptions be more objective and less distorted. *Cognitive defusion* is an example of a mindfulness technique since it requires a present-centered focus. For some people mindfulness is the key to overcoming the persistent negative thinking and emotional upset that leads to low self-esteem.

It might be helpful to think of the practice of cognitive defusion as developing an "observing head." Distancing yourself from your problems by objectively observing them can help you detach from your unhealthy thoughts. For example, your observing head can replace thoughts such as *I'm a jerk* with the thought *I am having the thought that I am a jerk*. This type of thinking helps us identify less with our skewed perceptions. We observe ourselves thinking a certain way rather than just plain thinking that way without questioning it. When we develop an observing head in this process of cognitive defusion, we mentally note our toxic thoughts rather than embrace them as true. We *observe* them rather than find ourselves in the throes of them.

Isn't it time to stop giving so much airtime to your unhealthy thoughts based on past conflicts or on fears of the future? Are you ready to practice strategies to help you live more fully *now* so you can witness your greatness instead?

GIVE IT A TRY

Visualization is a technique that can help you distance yourself from negative thoughts and limit their power over you.

Step 1: To defuse your unhealthy cognitions, visualize your thoughts and feelings as the weather. No matter how turbulent the hurricanes, blizzards, and rainstorms are, blue skies and balmy breezes will replace the turbulent weather if you are patient and have faith that the storm will pass. We don't try to change the weather—we cannot control it; rather, we can observe it and be detached from it, knowing the storm will pass and there will again be sunny days. Likewise, your disturbing thoughts will also pass, and by not reacting to the storm, you will develop equanimity and patience.

Step 2: Visualize your observing self as the sky and imagine putting your unwanted thoughts on a cloud. Do not try to alter the pace as they float by and do not let those thoughts distract you from being present-focused. Just observe those clouds disappearing with nonjudgmental awareness. You might find it helpful to draw some clouds on a piece of paper and write an upsetting thought on each one.

Step 3: Now imagine pushing a beach ball down in a body of water. It will keep popping back up. Likewise, when you resist your thoughts rather than accept them and move on, they will keep hitting you, like the ball popping back up. Take note of your anxieties instead of fighting against them—observe them without getting so attached to them. Have faith that you can handle anything that comes your way if you are accepting and mindful. You will have more inner strength and confidence if you stop sabotaging yourself by resisting and suppressing your thoughts or by speaking to yourself negatively.

Keep practicing visualizations such as these. The more you practice, the more you will make it a habit to look *at* your thoughts instead of *from* them. Take control of your thoughts instead of having them control you!

28: Practice Acceptance

"God grant me the serenity to accept the things I cannot change; courage to change the things I can; and wisdom to know the difference."

—Reinhold Niebuhr

We all have experienced the pain of being unable to change an outcome in our lives. For example, what parent has not tried to change a course for a child going on a self-destructive path? What accident victim has not replayed in their mind countless times the events leading up to the incident, plagued with thoughts of *If only I had…*? Who has not struggled with life's unfairness when we get more than our share of adversity, loss, and bad luck?

In the face of challenging and even traumatic situations that are beyond our ability to change, practicing the art of acceptance can be life-changing. Whether you have experienced the loss or death of a loved one, a malignant diagnosis, a painful breakup, or a life-altering disability, the more you are focused on the injustice of it all or how you failed to alter the course of your personal history, the more miserable you will be. Conversely, the more you accept what you have no power to change, the more you will rise above the trauma and make peace with it. Acceptance does not erase sadness and loss, but it does offer some inner peace. You might still experience pain, but you limit the suffering.

If you are spending too much time ruminating about what should or shouldn't be happening, maybe it's time to refocus your attention on what you can control instead of what you can't. Adopting an accepting attitude allows you to replace *Why is this happening to me—this is terrible!* with *It's unfortunate that this is happening to me, but I can handle it and can grow from it.*

GIVE IT A TRY

You can use coping statements to replace upsetting thoughts with thoughts of acceptance.

Step 1: Think of at least three disturbing thoughts that you tend to ruminate about. As a first step in working toward acceptance, consider these coping statements, all of which can serve as a mantra when you are struggling:

- *It is what it is.*

- *I can only change what is in my power to change.*

- *I can find meaning in any challenge or difficulty.*

- *There is no sense fighting against what is out of my control—I can only focus on what I can control.*

- *This is not about pointing the finger at myself or others—it is about acceptance, forgiveness, and coping.*

Step 2: Looking at the list, which coping statements do you find most beneficial? Can you add some others? Write down at least five coping statements that will help you work on practicing acceptance when you're coping with trauma and past events that continue to cause pain.

Step 3: Using note cards, write each of the coping statements from your list on separate cards. Carry these cards with you in your wallet, purse, or car, or keep them at your desk or kitchen counter. Refer to them regularly as you keep trying to incorporate mindfulness and acceptance into your day-to-day life. In difficult times these coping statements can help give you the support to stay emotionally stable.

Incorporating simple acceptance habits into your daily routine to replace judgmental thinking can help you finally embrace yourself so you can embrace your life. Isn't that worth some investment of your time and attention?

29: Transform Rumination into Mindful Thinking

"Mindfulness is paying attention on purpose, in the present moment, and nonjudgmentally, to the unfolding of experience moment to moment."

—Jon Kabat-Zinn

At one session my client, Gail, was very excited to report to me that she'd met the man of her dreams and had a wonderful few weeks in a new and promising relationship. She was excited to be in a relationship with someone she considered so special, and she decided to take it "one day at a time," enjoying the relationship without worrying about whether it would last. A few sessions later, though, she went back to being anxious and ruminative, despite the fact that things were going so well. She recalled times in the past when her relationships had failed and was afraid it would happen again. She reenacted in her mind how she had undermined her relationships and could not keep things together. She returned to the persistent worry that this new man would not like her the more he got to know her. She feared that it was just a matter of time before she would "screw up" the relationship, and she was anxious about making mistakes or saying something that might push him away.

Gail demonstrates the suffering that happens when we ruminate rather than think mindfully. Rumination focuses on negative events from the past that can't be changed, which will only keep you stuck in self-flagellation, leading to depression, anxiety, and low self-esteem. Going over the same negative thoughts in your head will take away your sense of power and control, since rumination focuses on the past and the uncertainty of the future, neither of which we have control over in the present.

What about you? Are you ready to incorporate more mindfulness strategies into your life for present-centered living? Isn't it time to transform your ruminative thoughts into more calming and present-focused mindful awareness?

GIVE IT A TRY

Mindful practices can get you in the habit of getting out of your head and into experiencing your life, which will help limit that negative self-talk that robs you of your self-esteem. Using a few practices that Jon Kabat-Zinn (2005) has popularized in his MBSR (mindfulness-based stress reduction) program will introduce you to some strategies you can incorporate into your daily routine.

Step 1: Take a raisin and instead of just popping it in your mouth, hold it for a few moments, noting the texture, feel, and look of the raisin. While you gaze at it, imagine you have never seen a raisin before and describe what you see. To highlight the sensation of touching the raisin, close your eyes and just feel the texture and sticky roughness. Then slowly put it in your mouth and, instead of eating it in the usual manner, spend a few minutes focusing on just that one raisin in your mouth, being aware of the sensations—noting the taste, smell, flavor as it slowly dissolves in your mouth with slow, deliberate chewing. As you finally swallow, note the sensation of the raisin going down your throat. This exercise can be done with any type of food and is a good way to help weight loss by slowing down your eating and being more mindful of what is going in your mouth!

Step 2: Give yourself a mindfulness tune-up with a *body scan*, a useful relaxation and mindfulness technique to calm the mind and body and create a present-centered awareness. In this practice lie down and progressively focus your attention on various parts of your body, from your toes through your left leg, to the right side and progressively up your body to your head. Gently shift your awareness to the sensations of each part of your body, noting and focusing on relaxing any tension you might feel. You can think of your body as an instrument and consider the body scan as a way to tune it.

Step 3: *Object meditation*—in which you spend a few moments observing and noting everyday objects—is another simple mindfulness practice you can incorporate in your daily routine. For example, instead of putting on a sweater almost automatically, spend a few moments feeling the texture, looking closely at the colors, touching the softness, noting the sensation on your fingers. Just like you did with the raisin, imagine you are seeing objects in your everyday life for the first time and take them in with all your senses.

There are numerous mindfulness practices that can help you focus your awareness on the present to get out of your head and immerse yourself in today. Mindful awareness is an investment in yourself. Aren't you worth it?

30: Cultivate a Beginner's Mind

"Be happy in the moment, that's enough.
Each moment is all we need, not more."

—Mother Teresa

If I told you that I missed my breakfast today, what would you think I meant? If you're like most people, you would think I skipped a meal and probably did not eat until lunchtime. However, I could say that I missed my breakfast simply because I was not paying attention to what I was eating. So how about you? Did you miss your breakfast today?

Modern mindfulness practice has its roots in an age-old concept from Zen Buddhism called the *beginner's mind*. When you have a beginner's mind, your mind is open without preconceptions and biases. Just think of a small child experiencing something for the first time. A small child is totally in the moment, taking life in with enthusiasm and openness, free from preconceived notions. As we get older, our memories, experiences, and biases taint our experience of the moment and interfere with a clear view of the present.

We are capable of a freshness of perspective, an absence of bias and stereotyping, and a lack of judgment about our experiences. When you have a beginner's mind, you are not held back by what happened in the past or what might happen in the future—you are open to what is happening in the moment without a cynical or jaded filter. Additionally, when we are mindful with a beginner's mind, we open our hearts. We can allow self-love to come in, instead of maintaining a self-critical perspective that fogs our worldview. When you see the world with fresh eyes, you can be more patient and accepting of how your life unfolds.

If some of your old ways of thinking and looking at the world haven't worked so well, isn't it time to give yourself another chance at cultivating the life you want and deserve? Are you ready to begin again with a "beginner's mind"?

GIVE IT A TRY

Having a beginner's mind will give you a fresh outlook on your life.

Step 1: Recall a child's innocence and freshness of perspective as they are discovering how the world works. Things we take for granted are not seen by young children in the same way—they are fascinated by what we often ignore, such as the beauty of a flower, the softness of the grass, the taste of their food.

Step 2: With the perspective of a young child, look at your surroundings. Instead of taking everything around you for granted, try to look at things as if you were seeing them for the first time. What do you see? What do you smell? What does it feel like?

What are your bodily sensations? What are you hearing? Notice the colors, shapes, textures, smells, and sounds around you.

Step 3: Observe the judgmental thoughts that go through your mind about what you are experiencing. For example, if you are in a room that is cluttered or has dirty dishes, you might tend to focus on what needs to be cleaned or picked up. Now look at the same things with a beginner's mind. Look at everything without value judgments and labels. Simply describe what you see, such as three dishes in the sink, some ketchup and crumbs on them, a blue edge around the rim.

Step 4: Now look in the mirror or at a picture of yourself and use the same beginner's mind perspective to view yourself. If you have low self-esteem, your descriptions of yourself will likely be negative. Many people focus on their flaws, such as a large nose or too many wrinkles. Replace those negatively biased descriptions with statements from the fresh perspective of a beginner's mind, with no judgments.

With a beginner's mind, your world of self-love will become open to you. Mindful awareness does not come naturally. As the old adage goes, practice makes perfect!

Embrace Self~Care

TAKING CHARGE OF YOURSELF

When it comes to self-care, think of what the flight attendant says in preparation for each flight: in the case of an emergency, everyone—including parents with small children—should put on their own oxygen mask first before attempting to help others.

In everyday life, though, parents often put themselves on such a back burner trying to tend to the needs of their children that they have little energy left for themselves at the end of the day. Working parents in particular try to make up for lost time, caring for everyone in the family except themselves after long hours at work.

Some people fear that too much focus on self-care is a form of selfishness. But self-care is not a selfish act—we need to be healthy in mind, body, and soul in order to be healthy for others. Taking good care of yourself will help you take better care of others. I have seen too many stressed-out people running on empty, and consequently, they really don't have the emotional bandwidth to truly be present-focused with others close to them.

Whether you are a caregiver or someone is caring for you, we all need to emotionally recharge and take care of ourselves. Just like our electronics need to be plugged in when they're running low on batteries, we need to give ourselves the time to emotionally recharge. Burnout happens when we give so much of ourselves that we end up feeling depleted and emotionally spent, leading to depression and apathy. Although we may have good intentions, when we are burned out, we end up having less to give to others. After all, you cannot give what you don't have yourself!

This chapter focuses on how to achieve a life balance, develop healthy self-care habits, set priorities, and take action to achieve goals. Making changes can be difficult, but by taking small actions instead of wide, sweeping ones, you are more likely to build on small successes.

Isn't it time to take care of yourself and take care of your life? You were given one life to live. If you don't take your self-care seriously, how in the world will you be able to truly embrace your greatness?

31: Make Yourself a Priority

"Love yourself first, and everything else falls in line. You really have to love yourself to get anything done in this world."

—Lucille Ball

Repeat after me: "I am important." Repeat this again: "I am important." In our busy lives with so much to do and so little time, we too often neglect our needs and put ourselves low on the totem pole of priorities. We treat ourselves like we are not important. While we juggle and multitask to "get it all done," we often find ourselves falling through the cracks.

Do you make yourself a priority with basic self-care? For example, do you go to the doctor for regular checkups, teeth cleanings, eye exams, and so forth? When we fit our needs around everyone else's, we often don't leave room to get healthy ourselves.

Self-care affects your self-esteem because if you think you are worth the effort, you will make your health a priority. And if you don't think you're worth it, take a leap of faith and trust me that you are. Self-care should not be seen as work and just one more thing on your plate; it's a path toward liberating yourself from self-doubt. One thing is for sure: when you neglect your own self-care, everything will suffer in the long run.

How about you? Do you treat yourself like an afterthought, or do you make yourself a priority? What's it going to take for you to really mean it when you say, "I am important"?

GIVE IT A TRY

Using some of the ideas in this section, find some time to make yourself a priority.

Step 1: List ten self-care goals that are important to you. Examples can range from committing yourself to exercise a few times a week to keeping a journal to help you explore your thoughts and feelings to setting aside more time on a regular basis to read more self-help books like this one.

Step 2: For each of those items on your list, write down an action you can do to honor that goal. For instance, write down specific daily or weekly goals that you can incorporate in your life to make yourself more of a priority. Start small so that you don't set yourself up to fail.

Step 3: To help you commit to the goals you set, it is helpful to do a *cost-benefit analysis* in which you evaluate the relative strengths and weaknesses of two or more alternatives in order to make a good decision. Start with a blank page in your journal or on your computer. On one side of the page list the costs of the chosen activity or choice, and on the other side write the advantages. To take the example of committing to exercising more, a "cost" would be having less time to watch TV after a hard day of work, and a benefit would be feeling better physically. When you look at your cost-benefit analysis, decide which column wins out for each item—the costs or the benefits.

Taking action to make yourself a priority is truly one of the best gifts you can give to yourself to get you on track to embrace your greatness. Are you ready?

32: Be Proactive

> *"There are people who make things happen, there are people who watch things happen, and there are people who wonder what happened. To be successful, you need to be a person who makes things happen."*
>
> —Jim Lovell

One of the most important elements of self-care is taking charge of yourself and your life, making things happen to go toward your goals. When we are *proactive*, we are empowered to adapt and go after our goals. We create opportunities and do not wait for them to come our way. We realize the degree of choice we have in creating our lives.

The opposite is being *reactive*. When we are reactive, we tend to blame and feel controlled by others, and we tend to wait for life to give us what we want rather than taking charge of satisfying our wants and needs.

People with a high degree of healthy self-esteem tend to be proactive, whereas those with a victim mentality, who feel controlled by factors outside of themselves, tend to be reactive. The mentality and self-talk of a proactive person differ from a reactive person, in that proactive people think and talk in what I refer to as "victor" language, as opposed to the reactive person's "victim" language.

Notice the difference:

Reactive Victim Self-Talk	Proactive Victor Self-Talk
Blames others	Takes personal responsibility for choices
"I can't."	"I can."
"I should."	"I will."
"I have to."	"I choose to."
"If only…"	"Only if…"
"He made me cry."	"I cried when he said that."
"I wish I had a better job."	"I need to learn to be more satisfied with my job or look for another one."

By learning to transform your self-talk from victim language to victor language, you can shift from "can't" to "can" and "should" to "will."

How about you? Do you tend to be more proactive or reactive? Do you make things happen, or do you wait for them to happen? If you tend to be more reactive, isn't it time to take control of your life?

GIVE IT A TRY

Thinking in proactive ways can empower you to take charge of your life instead of being a victim of circumstance. Proactivity is something that can be learned and practiced.

Step 1: Look at the previous list differentiating reactive victim self-talk from proactive victor self-talk. What sounds more like you? Reflect on these two alternatives. Do you tend to blame others for things that go wrong in your life, or do you take responsibility for your choices?

Step 2: For any items that fall under reactive self-talk, rephrase them into proactive self-talk alternatives. Can you appreciate which way of thinking is more positive and can lead to more solutions than problems?

Step 3: Think of the challenges in your life and what you tell yourself about these challenges. Do you dig yourself deeper into holes with your victim-like mentality? Write down these challenging situations in the format shown previously, first using your victim self-talk, then transforming it into victor self-talk. For example, *If only I had a more sensitive spouse* can be changed to *I need to be stronger in setting limits when my spouse is not sensitive*. Notice that "have/had" self-talk language is reactive and "be" phrases are more proactive; they are action-oriented. Victim self-talk often entails waiting for the other person to change, whereas focusing on what you can be or do reflects healthier victor self-talk.

When you are proactive, you will feel more empowered and in control of your life. You have a lot at stake—don't let anyone take that from you by being a victim instead of a victor!

33: Set Goals for Mind-Body Balance

"Health and well-being are the natural state of the body and the mind."

—Deepak Chopra

Even though we often refer to the mind and the body as two separate entities, the mind and body are really two sides of the same coin. Looking at things differently is not enough to improve self-esteem—action must be taken.

If you take care of your body, your mind benefits and you feel good about yourself. A wealth of research has pointed to the fact that the chemicals in the brain that are released during exercise, such as endorphins and cortisol, are physiologically mood-boosting. The mind and body are very much intertwined and work together to create our moods and thoughts. In case you need more convincing of the importance of the mind-body connection, just think of the visceral reaction you have when you witness something that makes you queasy.

For those with low self-esteem, even the thought of speaking up during a meeting, never mind being the presenter in front of your peers and clients, will be enough to get your head pounding, heart racing, body sweating, and stomach in knots. On the positive side, think of your heart palpitating when you see your crush come into a room, when you fall in love, or when you hold your baby or grandchild for the first time. Learning to be aware of and appreciating the importance of this mind-body connection will help you be comfortable in your own skin.

Take time to make your mental as well as physical health a priority. Your self-esteem will blossom!

GIVE IT A TRY

When you focus on improving your body as well as your mind, you will appreciate how the mind and body work together to create growth and healing.

Step 1: Ask yourself:

- *What are my goals to improve my mind-body connection?*

- *Do I make my physical self-care a priority?*

- *Am I too busy for exercise or planning meals to eat better?*

- *Do I use food, alcohol, or other substances in excess to feel good rather than body movement, stretching, meditation, or exercise?*

Step 2: Consider how you can prioritize your life differently to make room for self-care. List some goals to improve your mind and your body and how they work together.

Step 3: Instead of thinking in vague terms like *I need to exercise more*, make your goals specific and break them into phases. To help you get started, make a behavioral log to track your progress—you can have a page for each of the individual goals you are working on. For each day that you complete the planned activity, make a check mark in your log, and at the end of a given time period, reward yourself if you met your goal. The reward could be buying that sweater you've eyed online or going to that movie you've wanted to see. Here is how your two-week chart could look:

Mind-Body Behavior Log		
Goal #1: Exercise at least 3 times per week		
Ways to accomplish goal: walking, swimming, taking a class at the gym		
Completed goal = 6 checkmarks in 2 weeks		
Reward earned = _____		
	Week 1	Week 2
Monday		
Tuesday	✓	✓
Wednesday		✓
Thursday	✓	
Friday		✓
Saturday	✓	
Sunday	✓	✓

Reward yourself by completing your goals on a behavior chart like this one. You deserve it!

34: Get Your Life in Balance

"Life is like riding a bicycle. To keep your balance, you must keep moving."

—Albert Einstein

What drives you? What motivates you? What are your values and goals? What are you committed to that provides you with true life meaning? All too often these questions take a backseat to the practicalities of the day—working, going to school, eating, taking care of pets and children, attending to your basic needs. However, your life values and general sense of commitment are like the glue that makes your day-to-day life activities meaningful. Part of taking care of yourself is making sure your life choices are aligned with your overall values.

Using a pie chart is a great way to visualize your self-care needs, goals, and values, and how they fit in with your life choices in the way you are living your life at present. Pie chart visuals are just as useful in the areas of self-help and psychotherapy as in the business world to clarify your values and goals and to get a snapshot of how you measure up with how you want to live your life.

Following are two pie charts representing John's life, four years into starting his own business. As you can see, his actual life is out of whack. By spending so much time and energy making sure his business doesn't fail, he's neglected the rest of his life, such as exercise, socializing with friends, and relaxing with other interests and hobbies. He has disengaged from his social circle, dated very infrequently, and made little time for anything other than his start-up. Notice the differences in the two charts depicting his actual behavior and his ideal goal.

Actual Life Balance

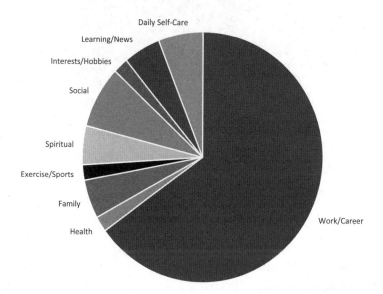

Ideal Life Balance

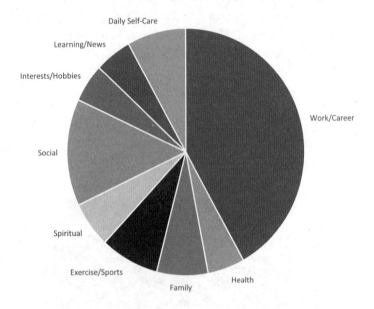

How about you? Are your slices of life closely aligned with your ideal life balance, or do you need to reprioritize how you spend your time?

GIVE IT A TRY

Achieving a life balance is a universal issue that most of us are constantly readjusting. Using a visual tool will get your actual and ideal priorities more in sync by letting you clearly see what areas you'd like to change.

Step 1: Take an inventory of your own actual versus ideal life balance. Start by making a list of all the areas in your life you devote time to. On the next page is what John's original list looked like, but feel free to substitute categories of your own.

John's Actual Life Balance	
Work/Career	65%
Health	2%
Family	5%
Exercise/Sports	2%
Spiritual	5%
Social	8%
Interests/Hobbies	2%
Learning/News	5%
Daily Self-Care	6%
Total	**100%**

Make two versions of this list, labeling one **My Actual Balance** and the other **My Ideal Balance**. Then assign percentages to each area, the first set representing your actual present life and the second set representing how you'd like your life to be (but with both sets, of course, totaling 100 percent).

Step 2: Now create a pie chart (or other graphical depiction) based on each list using your computer's word processor so you have a visual tool to get a clearer picture of how your actual and ideal goals differ. Is there a big difference between what is actually happening and what you would like to happen? What would you like to devote more of your waking hours to, and what would you like to spend less time doing? This analysis can help you establish priorities.

Step 3: You can use the pie chart model in other areas of your life as well, to reestablish your general priorities or more intangible goals. For example, you might find it helpful to clarify your values instead of your time allotments; if so, sample entries could include giving to others through acts of kindness; practicing meditation, yoga, and self-rejuvenation; and getting involved in your church or synagogue.

It's time to take control of your life, so you will be more likely to love yourself and love your life!

35: Develop Small Mini-Habits for Lasting Change

"It's not what we do once in a while that shapes our lives. It's what we do consistently over time."

—Anthony Robbins

Are you looking to have better health habits, get fit, get your home organized, tackle a household project, or overcome procrastination? Do you have assignments, projects, or upcoming tests that you are having trouble preparing for? Are you having trouble even getting motivated to start?

No matter how important the goal is to you, life often gets in the way. It's hard to turn our goals into reality when we have so much to do and so little time. You think it would be easier to make more informed choices nowadays with all the information we have available at our fingertips, whether it's the nutritional value of some food we want to look up on Google or a DIY video on YouTube. With our tablets and smartphone apps, we can find all sorts of helpful aids to achieve our goals. Sometimes they do help, like when we can track our steps daily. However, as with almost everything, there is a downside. Technology can be a supreme distraction, with our time being sucked up by checking our e-mail umpteen times a day, surfing the web, playing online games, and so on.

Given such busy lives and so many distractions, how can we stay motivated, focus on our goals, be productive, overcome procrastination, and maximize our potential? Think mini-habits!

Stephen Guise (2013) offers us a no-fail solution to help us get motivated to make minor and major life changes through developing mini-habits, which are habits we create in our lives that are "too small to fail." Guise suggests you make your goals "stupid small" so you are bound to succeed in changing behaviors. He uses himself as an example. In his quest to jump-start a personal fitness program, he gave himself the "one push-up challenge." No matter how unmotivated he was, he managed to get in one push-up a day, and any push-ups after that he called the "bonus round." Starting small with mini-habits ends up reaping big gains by developing into more in-depth adjustments that lead to lasting change.

Are you ready to develop some mini-habits to jump-start your goals? Are you ready to go after the life you want and deserve?

GIVE IT A TRY

Getting yourself motivated with small mini-goals can help you start making changes to empower yourself to take control of your life.

Step 1: Write out at least three goals you have that you're having trouble getting started with, such as writing a book, losing weight, eating more nutritiously, organizing a closet, cleaning the basement, making more friends, studying for a test, or completing a project or assignment.

Step 2: For each of your goals write out at least one mini-habit that can help you get a start on it. For example, Guise set the goal of writing fifty words a day on his new book. Even though he ended up writing more, his extremely attainable goal of only fifty words a day got him motivated to get involved in and committed to his project. Be specific about the parameters of your mini-habits:

- For each mini-habit write down what time of day you will do it.

- Write down how many times a week you will do it.

- Set a time limit for it, such as a week or a month, in which you regularly do this habit.

Remember, even if you break the ice with only one mini-habit you commit to, you can still add some "bonus rounds"— you don't have to stop at one mini-habit, but you can.

Step 3: Plan a time in the future to review your new mini-habit routine. For example, if you committed to write down one thing you are grateful for each day, after a month read over what you logged and assess if this mini-habit is accomplishing what you wanted it to. If it is, commit to keep doing it; if you're ready for more, increase your goal to write two or more things each day.

Step 4: Reward yourself for your progress each time you perform a mini-habit. Something as simple as saying *"Yay, go me!"* can help keep you motivated. Or give yourself a hug (or, in this case, a mini-hug!). Those little bits of action and self-kindness can go a long way.

Keep in mind that mini-habits can help you make major changes in your life. Aren't you worth it?

8

Embrace Assertiveness

SPEAKING UP AND SETTING LIMITS

Perhaps one of the most important predictors of happiness and a sense of well-being is having a strong support network. That does not just happen. People who are good at developing a strong support system are able to communicate in a way that brings people closer to them. Conversely, those who communicate insensitively, or those who distance and protect themselves from others due to self-doubt, will have trouble making strong and healthy connections.

If you have low self-esteem, you might find that in your attempts to avoid the possibility of rejection, you end up pushing people away, leading to isolation and loneliness. Social anxiety and taking yourself too seriously will make it hard for people to feel close and connected—it keeps people at a distance. Underlying this protectiveness is a whole host of irrational beliefs and unhealthy behaviors that isolate you from others. What is meant to be self-protective actually backfires and makes you feel worse about yourself and more alone.

Learning healthy communication skills reaps huge benefits in terms of both helping you build self-esteem and helping improve your ability to connect with others. Communication is something we all do—it is so basic and necessary—but most of us never learn the guidelines for healthy communication. Wouldn't it be great if it were part of every school curriculum, right up there with math, spelling, and science?

Being able to distinguish between the three major types of communication—*assertive*, *nonassertive*, and *aggressive*—helps us communicate effectively, and learning the guidelines for each type can be eye-opening. I often have found role-playing to be quite helpful with my clients to put into practice new assertive skills, and you can do that in front of a mirror or with a trusted friend, family member, or, of course, a therapist. In this chapter I have highlighted some important hallmarks of healthy communication.

36: Develop Assertive Skills

"Assertive behavior is a positive self-affirmation which also values the other people in your life."

—Robert Alberti and Michael Emmons

Imagine that three coworkers are all part of a larger workplace team meeting, where the topic turns to a difficult client's behavior that morning. Coworker A exclaims, "He is just trying to pick a fight! What a jerk! He should know that is no way to talk to us!" Coworker B follows up with, "I certainly did not appreciate him acting disrespectfully to us, and we need to decide how to set limits on disrespectful behavior from our clients." Coworker C nods her head and does not offer anything, for fear of saying the wrong thing and sounding stupid.

These differing styles are examples of the three main types of communication, with coworker A displaying aggressive communication, coworker B displaying assertive communication, and coworker C displaying nonassertive communication. It is important to understand the difference in order to develop healthy relationships. Low self-esteem is correlated with nonassertive and aggressive behavior, whereas assertive communication conveys self-confidence and a positive self-view.

Just think how much easier it would be to embrace your greatness if you were not afraid to assert yourself. Isn't it time to find your voice?

GIVE IT A TRY

Understanding the three types of communication will help you identify your communication style and those of others, which is the first step to asserting yourself.

Step 1: Write out some examples of ways you have acted or things you have said in times of conflict or stress that demonstrate each of the three types of communication. Make sure you include a sample statement for each scenario.

Step 2: For each of the nonassertive and aggressive statements you wrote, think of a way to transform them into assertive statements, like these (note that assertive statements virtually always include "I"):

"You" Statements	"I" Statements
"He makes me so mad!"	"I am mad at him when he acts rude to me."
"You aren't listening to me!"	"I don't think I am getting my point across."
"You shouldn't say that to me."	"I feel disrespected when you say that to me."
"Don't you ever say that again!"	"I ask you not to say that again—it is hurtful."

An example of a nonassertive statement is telling someone "I don't care" when you really do care. You can make the decision to focus on being honest and direct rather than hiding your feelings. As a foundation you need to first identify how *you* feel and what *you* think instead of worrying what *they* feel and think.

Step 3: As you go about your everyday life, pay attention to how you and others come across. Try to identify "I" statements and "you" statements, challenging yourself to turn your own aggressive or nonassertive statements into healthier ways of communicating. Remember that honesty and tactful directness are the hallmarks of assertive communication. Being able to identify in yourself and others the three types of communication approaches will be important in removing any communication blocks that get in the way of developing a healthy network.

Assertive "I" statements will help you develop confidence, get closer to others, and truly embrace the life you want to live!

37: Control Your Anger

"Whatever is begun in anger ends in shame."

—Benjamin Franklin

Anger can be an adaptive reaction to what is unfair and unjust. However, we too often let anger control us rather than taking control of our anger. We all feel angry sometimes—anger is an important emotion that signals when things are not fair or when we are not being treated the way we deserve. But feeling angry does not justify aggressive behavior.

Do you find yourself arguing with others close to you to prove that you are right, then justifying it as "expressing yourself"? That's basically the definition of an argument. When you try to change someone's mind, you might not realize your goal is an aggressive one. In contrast, an assertive goal would be to express yourself without trying to change another person, even if what you're trying to change is just their perception. The truth is, you can change someone's reality, but you can never change their perceptions!

If you have low self-esteem, you likely have little confidence in expressing yourself and are afraid of making waves or getting someone upset. Low self-esteem plants the seeds of out-of-control anger, as the tendency to keep things inside builds tension, and the simmering anger ends up exploding at some point or turning inward to depression. Learning to control intense emotions is an important skill on the road to developing self-empowerment and self-love.

"Anger" is one letter short of "danger"—watch out for letting your anger control you instead of you controlling it!

GIVE IT A TRY

Having the ability to self-soothe and calm yourself in the height of anger or any other strong, distressing emotion can be achieved by learning better coping skills to handle intense feelings.

Step 1: Reflect on these questions and write out your answers, referring to them in times of need:

- *How can I develop the confidence to be more assertive in expressing myself so that anger does not build up?*

- *Am I expressing my anger assertively, or am I so overwhelmed with emotion that I am expressing it aggressively?*

- *Do I attempt to suppress my anger rather than acknowledge it as a normal emotion that can be expressed assertively?*

- *When I'm dealing with someone I'm angry at, do I strive to be kind, or do I try to be right?*

Step 2: In the height of anger use coping cards to help calm yourself down. Examples of self-coping statements to write on the cards include:

- *No one controls my anger except me.*

- *She does not make me so mad; rather, I get mad when she criticizes me.*

- *When I feel out of control, I will make an effort to try to not control others.*

- *It's okay to feel angry, but that does not mean I have a right to act aggressively. The first is a feeling, the second is a behavior.*

Step 3: Assemble a "calming toolbox" to help you handle anger. Include items from your mindfulness toolbox (from tip #26 earlier) and the coping cards from step 2 above. Here are some additional toolbox ideas that can help de-escalate angry thoughts:

- A small notebook to journal your feelings

- A small bottle of bubbles to remind you to "lighten up"

- Metaphorical items like a crayon to put color into your thoughts rather than hanging on to black-and-white thinking

- A small magnifying glass to remind you to be a thought detective and identify any unhelpful thoughts

- A toy stop sign to visualize the word STOP when it is best to not react in the height of anger

- A green light to replace the stop sign, when you express yourself assertively and confidently

Taking control of your anger before it controls you will lead to self-empowerment that will help you embrace your greatness!

38: Use Active Listening Skills

"We know that when people learn to communicate effectively with each other, their lives and their relationships can be truly transformed."

—Thomas Gordon

As subtle as the distinction might seem, the difference between *hearing* and *listening* makes all the difference in the world in determining whether or not you communicate well. Learning the art of listening can be one of the greatest gifts you ever give to others—it shows respect and validation, and your relationships will more likely be good ones.

What is the difference between hearing and listening? Thomas Gordon (1977) coined the term "active listening" to differentiate it from hearing. He regarded merely hearing as passively taking in audible sounds, without necessarily looking behind the words to see what message is being conveyed. In contrast, he regarded listening as requiring more effort and concentration. Taking it one step further, active listening entails not just saying "uh-huh" and letting the other person talk without feedback, but instead offering words that show empathy and clarification and restating what you hear—all of which is validating to the other person. When you actively listen, you take into account the feelings behind the words without trying to show the other person how wrong they are.

Being able to differentiate hearing from listening is an important step to improve your communication skills and find your assertive voice.

Hearing	Active Listening
Passive	Paraphrases, summarizes, interprets
Focused on being heard	Focused on understanding
Can be judgmental	Shows empathy and acceptance of others
Talks *at*	Talks *with*
Takes in audible sounds	Requires more action
Can be invalidating	Is validating to others
Commanding, "telling it like it is"	Reflecting, offering feedback
Threatening, persuading, ordering	Accepting, tolerant, flexible
Leads to arguments and conflict	Leads to supportive, positive relationships

What about you? Are you an active listener? Or do you tend just to "hear"? Does your self-consciousness limit your ability to truly listen to others over your own internal self-talk? Do you give your self-doubting thoughts too much airtime?

GIVE IT A TRY

The art of listening is an important skill to have not only in being more connected to others, but also in being more connected to a healthy self.

Step 1: Look at the two lists above that distinguish hearing from active listening and reflect on your own communication style. Do you tend to listen…or do you just hear? Here is a rule of thumb if you have trouble differentiating between the two: If you are in an argument with someone, chances are you are just hearing and not really listening. Likewise, if you tend to remain quiet and refrain from giving feedback and clarification while someone is talking, you are likely hearing more than listening.

Step 2: Identify and write down some statements you recall saying that reflect hearing instead of listening. How can you change them around to show more reflection, validation, and summarizing? For example, if you remember saying to a loved one, "*Get over it,*" you can change this invalidating statement to: "*It sounds really tough for you—how frustrating!*"

Step 3: Keep in mind that when you are more accepting of yourself and less judgmental, you are more likely to be accepting of others. Ask yourself, *Am I more interested in being* right *or in being* kind?

Choose kindness over being right! You can't go wrong—and you'll be right every time!

39: Communicate with Self-Respect, Not Self-Deprecation

"Respect yourself and others will respect you."

—Confucius

Dennis used an interesting type of humor when talking about himself to his coworkers. He was the first to point out his idiosyncrasies and laugh them off, as if they were a source of amusement. He enjoyed the attention and chuckles he got from others and took their laughter as a sign that they liked him and enjoyed being with him. Even though he was poking fun at himself, he saw this as a way to be likable and disarming.

Dennis did not realize that his sarcastic and self-degrading humor actually showed aggression and belittling toward himself. Sarcasm, whether directed toward yourself or others, is actually aggression disguised as humor. There is really nothing funny about it! When you have low self-esteem, you tend to feel inadequate. So despite the fact that you are sensitive to the rejection and disapproval of others, you might feel much freer to be insulting toward yourself. It's like you are beating someone to the punch—putting yourself down before they have a chance to!

How about you? Do you communicate in a way that is self-deprecatory? If so, isn't it time that you start treating yourself with more respect?

GIVE IT A TRY

When you communicate to others like you are nothing special, chances are both you and the other person will agree. By coming across like you think you are special, chances are you'll both agree on that also.

Step 1: Reflect on the way you project yourself to others and ask yourself if you demonstrate a lack of self-esteem by any of the following:

- Not speaking up when you have something to say

- Self-deprecating humor

- Poor eye contact

- Trailing voice

- Nervous mannerisms

- Too many "I'm sorry's"

- Inability to accept compliments

- Shyness

- Poor body language, like slouching and looking down

Do you identify with any of these? Observe yourself over the next couple weeks, and when you notice yourself displaying these traits, work to correct them. It might be hard to change habits, but awareness is the first step.

Step 2: It will be almost impossible to change your behaviors until you do some inner work on changing your internal communication. Here are a couple of examples of how you can transform negative self-talk in order to embrace your greatness:

- If you have the thought *I am inferior,* change it to: *I am as worthy as everyone else.* This will help you challenge the basic premise of not being "good enough," allowing you to express your opinion and thoughts more freely.

- If you tend to overapologize, make a conscious effort to stop saying "I'm sorry" when you did not do anything wrong.

Old habits are hard to break, but keep trying to change those self-downing messages that keep your self-esteem on shaky ground. Instead of putting yourself down and showing disrespect to yourself, be your best cheerleader!

40: Identify Your Assertive Bill of Rights

"To deny people their human rights is to challenge their very humanity."

—Nelson Mandela

One of the most surprising questions that clients have asked me throughout the years is whether they have a right to feel or think in a certain way. I've heard all of these and more: "Do I really have a right to feel this way?" "Isn't it selfish to say what I want or need?" "Do I have a right to speak up?" "Do I have a right to say no?" "To be a good person, shouldn't I focus on what others want instead of what I want?"

It is impossible to be confident and assertive if you don't accept the basic premise that you have a right to feel your feelings and think your thoughts. If you don't allow yourself these basic rights, you end up embracing your shamefulness instead of your greatness.

Of course, with all rights come corresponding responsibilities. For example:

Basic Assertive Rights	Corresponding Responsibilities
I have a right to speak my mind.	*I have a responsibility to value and accept the opinions of others nonjudgmentally.*
I have a right to set boundaries and limits.	*I will respect the limits and boundaries of others.*
I have a right to make mistakes.	*I need to be accepting of the mistakes of others with kindness.*

Don't you—and others—deserve respect and to stand up for your basic human rights? By identifying your rights and corresponding responsibilities, everyone wins!

GIVE IT A TRY

Respecting yourself by identifying your basic assertive rights will put to rest the notion that you do not deserve to think or feel a certain way.

Step 1: To help you identify and embrace your fundamental human rights, first look at this list. Ask yourself if you personally accept these basic assertive rights:

- *I have a right to say no.*

- *I have a right to be treated with respect.*

- *I have a right to speak up, even if others do not agree or like what I have to say.*

- *I have a right to make my needs as important as others' needs.*

- *I have a right to my opinions.*

- *I have a right to make mistakes and even fail.*

- *I have a right to not meet others' expectations of me that are unreasonable.*

- *I have a right to set healthy boundaries and limits with others.*

- *I have a right to ask for help.*

- *I have a right to not be "superman" or "superwoman."*

Step 2: From this list identify any of the rights that you have trouble accepting.

Step 3: Using this list as a springboard, write out your own "Assertive Bill of Rights." It can remind you of your undeniable personal rights, which will serve as a cornerstone to improving self-acceptance and confidence. Keep it in a prominent place, such as by your computer, to remind yourself often of your rights.

Step 4: For each item in your personal bill of rights write a corresponding responsibility.

Step 5: Imagine for a moment what life would be like if you accepted these basic assertive rights unconditionally, along with your responsibilities. How would you feel differently about yourself? How would you feel differently about others?

Once you have embraced your basic human rights—and corresponding responsibilities—you will have a solid foundation to truly embrace your own greatness!

9

Embrace Healthy Relationships

ENLISTING SUPPORT FOR A HEALTHY YOU

Healthy relationships are important in creating a healthy you. No matter if you are introverted or extroverted, social connection and having loving relationships are crucial to development. Having a healthy support system will provide you with a loving foundation of growth. The greater your sense of social support, the better you'll feel about yourself and the more trusting and optimistic you'll feel about your life. Those who have at least one person they can confide in—with whom they can share their innermost thoughts and feelings—are generally happier people.

Sometimes we find ourselves in relationships that work against us rather than for us. Of course, if you are in abusive or toxic relationships that do not support your growth, it will increase your self-doubt, low self-esteem, and fear of the outside world. In toxic relationships it is important to learn to set limits on how the unhealthiness affects you, to the point that some relationships are best severed. When dealing with loved ones with whom you cannot physically sever ties, such as children or parents, learning to set good boundaries is of utmost importance.

In this chapter we will focus on how to overcome approval addiction and forgive others so you can find peace. We will focus on how healthy social support can help you deal with stress, in part through what's been termed the "tend-and-befriend response" in a research study led by psychologist Shelley Taylor (2000). We will also learn from Kelly McGonigal (2016) about the importance of developing "bigger-than-yourself" goals, in which personal goals that include connecting with or service to others actually help us personally to grow and establish a life of meaning and connection.

So are you ready to improve your social support system? If you find yourself feeling isolated, alone, or misunderstood, isn't it time to both seek and give support so that you can grow through relationships?

41: Break the Habit of Approval Addiction

"A man cannot be comfortable without his own approval."

—Mark Twain

Do you find yourself preoccupied with how you come across to others? If you are overly critical of yourself and have a hard time accepting and loving yourself *as you are right now,* looking outward for the love and approval you lack from within will be an impossible task. No amount of approval from others will replace self-love. You'll never get enough, and there's always a sense that you're just waiting for the other shoe to drop, when you will be met with rejection or disapproval. That is why those who lack self-love often develop some form of social anxiety, putting too much emphasis on what other people think of them.

One young adult client of mine stuttered when he was anxious and even developed mild panic attacks while talking to others, fearing that they would think he sounded "dumb" or "boring." He claimed he felt like an "approval addict"—needing a "fix" of approval from his fellow students or professors to feel okay about himself. In his case, as in the case of many who suffer from social anxiety and low self-esteem, to complicate matters his perceptions became very distorted and he actually perceived criticism and rejection even when there wasn't any. On the days

Embrace Healthy Relationships

he felt more insecure, just a glance, comment, or expression from someone could be twisted as a sign of disapproval. Recently, just seeing his friend looking down at his phone while talking to him threw him into a self-esteem crisis.

How about you—are you looking for love in all the wrong places? Does your approval addiction get in the way of thinking clearly and expressing yourself? Remember that when you look for approval from others, you are minimizing the importance of your own self-love.

GIVE IT A TRY

Breaking the habit of looking to others for approval will increase your own sense of self-approval.

Step 1: If you find yourself even slightly approval-addicted, ask yourself these questions:

- *What do I hope they think of me?*

- *What would it mean about myself if they do not like me?*

- *Am I looking for the approval from others that I need to get from myself?*

- *Why do I value the opinions of others more than my own opinion of myself?*

- *What am I looking for outwardly that I need to feel from within?*

Step 2: Identify some of your core beliefs and self-statements that underlie your need for approval. For example, *If she rejects me, then that means I am not likable.* Now ask yourself if each statement you identify is true.

Step 3: Challenge those core self-statements that are not true with something more accurate. For example, *It would be terrible if she does not like me* can be changed to *I would be disappointed if she does not like me.* This takes away the absolute, all-or-nothing way of looking at the situation and replaces it with a more flexible perception that does not make or break your self-view.

Step 4: Once you identify the negative thoughts that underlie your approval addiction and replace all-or-nothing thoughts with more rational and flexible thoughts, make an action plan to reclaim your own sense of self-love and respect. For instance, instead of wanting others to think you are interesting, make a plan of how you can expand your knowledge and activities to find *yourself* more interesting!

By challenging the need for approval to feel good about yourself, you will be able to really love yourself, flaws and all.

42: Develop a Support Network

"A friend is one that knows you as you are, understands where you have been, accepts what you have become, and still, gently allows you to grow."

—Elbert Hubbard

The quality of your relationships in some degree corresponds to the quality of your life. If you have low self-esteem, you are more likely to distrust people, since your foundation of trust in yourself is shaky, which makes you self-protective.

All too often fear of disapproval, ridicule, rejection, or just "not fitting in" ends up making you more and more isolated. To ward off fears of rejection or disapproval, you ironically end up being more self-critical as well as critical of others, which is hardly really protecting yourself. You might be protecting yourself from others, but you are not protecting you from yourself! What is meant to be protective becomes self-imposed isolation.

It might not come as a surprise to learn that research has found differences in men and women when it comes to social connectedness. On average men typically become more competitive rather than cooperative in times of stress. Women, however, are more likely to reach out for social support and nurturing, a process that researcher Shelley Taylor (2002) calls the "tend-and-befriend response."

Although women might be more biologically wired for connection, it does not mean that social support is any less important for men. Study after study of both men and women has shown that strength of social connection is one of the best predictors of happiness—in fact, it's often the singular most important factor.

How about you? What is the quality of your support network? If your support system is lacking, isn't it time to reach out and improve your social connections? Your emotional and physical health depend on it!

GIVE IT A TRY

Do you tend to isolate and hunker down in times of stress, or do you tend to befriend? Your choice might affect not only your level of happiness, but your health and longevity as well!

Step 1: Reflect on the following questions. As usual, writing down your answers in your journal will help you gain more clarity and lead to bigger changes.

- *Are you happy with the quality of your support system? How could it be better?*

- *Do you have at least one person you can confide in? Write down the people you can confide in, and if you do not have any, explain why.*

- *If you are unhappy with your support system, can you identify why you are having trouble fostering connections? What gets in the way? List at least two reasons.*

- *What are some practical strategies that you can use to create more connections? List at least two actionable goals, such as a joining an interest-related club.*

Step 2: Make a list of the possible groups, events, clubs, classes, and so forth that you can join to improve your social connectedness. Each week commit yourself to trying at least one thing that is new or different. Not everything will work, but if you keep trying, something will stick!

Step 3: Enlist the support of others you do have in your life at present. Share your journey with at least one of these people and ask for their help in keeping you on track. The idea is that you don't have to go it alone! Just reaching out for help, which is hard for many people with low self-esteem, will help you derive the strength to keep moving forward. Besides, research has found that even just the act of telling someone about what you plan to do increases the chances that you'll actually do it!

Making social connections is not easy for many people who have low self-esteem. It takes courage to forge new relationships and open yourself up to let people in. Getting out of your comfort zone will be an important step in enlisting a supportive network, which in turn will help you be healthier in mind as well as in body!

43: Treat Others with Loving-Kindness and Compassion

"Be kind, for everyone you meet is fighting a harder battle."

—Plato

In chapter 5 we focused on treating ourselves with kindness and self-compassion. Now we'll extend that same sense of loving-kindness and compassion to others. Being able to forgive and have compassion for others, even if they have hurt you, will free you from the chains of bitterness and resentment. This is not to condone bad behavior or lessen your hurt—it is just that you deserve better than to hang on to negativity and bitterness by giving so much power to others.

Treating others with as much loving-kindness as possible has benefits. First of all, if you are loving and kind to others, you will be more likely to receive loving-kindness from others. As the saying goes, you get more flies with honey than with vinegar. People who are positive tend to attract positive people. People who are critical, negative, and judgmental tend to push people away, leading to isolation and conflict-ridden relationships.

Are you ready to heal yourself with thoughts of love and kindness to everyone, including you?

GIVE IT A TRY

When you focus on kindness and compassion toward others, you focus on being kind rather than being right.

Step 1: Imagine putting your fingers in a Chinese finger trap and pulling outward from each side; as you may recall, your fingers get more stuck the more you pull. This is analogous to what happens when we try to be right rather than kind. When we try to prove our point or change someone's mind, we often end up in conflict with others since our goal is self-righteous instead of loving.

Step 2: Now imagine pushing your fingers toward each other to release the trap. That is how you can visualize freeing yourself from relationship conflicts: when you move toward another person in kindness rather than pulling away from them to prove how right you are, you're out of the trap of conflict!

Step 3: Think of a person in your life with whom you have a problematic relationship. Think of two recent examples of conflict with this person. Write down what your goal was during the conflict—to show them you were right and to change their mind and see it your way, or was your goal to be kind, compromise, and express yourself with no strings attached?

Step 4: If your interaction with this person were guided by kindness rather than righteousness, how would your relationship be different? Journaling the answers to some of these questions can be helpful:

- *How would you feel differently about the other person?*

- *Would you focus on setting better limits?*

- *How would you feel differently about yourself?*

- *Would you be more forgiving?*

- *Would you be more loving?*

- *Would you feel closer to others?*

- *Would you personally feel happier?*

Next time you are stuck in a trap, think of allowing yourself to feel kindness so you can enjoy warmer and closer relationships with others.

44: Give Others the Gift of Forgiveness

"Forgiveness says you are given another chance to make a new beginning."

—Desmond Tutu

There are a multitude of ways that people feel wronged, whether we experience small slights or real trauma and abuse. Sometimes life itself is very cruel, and we find it hard to forgive life for giving us what we think we never should have had to handle. Sometimes people hurt us in a way we don't want or deserve, and we become defined by bitterness and "How could they?" indignation.

As much as we rail against the unfairness of it all, there is one thing for sure: the path to peace and healing is never paved with bitterness. When we are unforgiving, it becomes more about us than anyone else. We can't change what has happened to us, just like we can't undo our own behaviors and choices that we have a hard time forgiving. The only thing we *can* change is our response to what has happened. Our response is a choice, and it will determine if we remove the chains of the past by learning from it or if we stay chained to the past by living in it.

Here are some truths about forgiveness to clarify some common misperceptions:

- Forgiving does not mean that *they* were *right* and *you* were *wrong*. Some people hold on to the sense of righteousness way past the point of usefulness.

- Forgiveness is much more about you than about the other person. Your own thoughts of bitterness now are holding you back.

- When you forgive others, you stop expecting them to give you something they don't have to give.

- The word "forgive" can be broken down into two others: "for" and "give." *Give* yourself the ability to move *for*ward.

Have you been held back by bitterness and grudges? Isn't it time to give the gift of forgiveness to yourself? Even if you don't think another person deserves your forgiveness, don't *you* deserve it?

GIVE IT A TRY

Holding on to negativity appears on the surface to put others down while it elevates you, but it actually works in the opposite way: the more you hold grudges, the more the bitterness will hold you back from being happier with yourself.

Step 1: Read the points listed above about forgiveness and spend a few moments writing down how they relate to you. What do you find so hard to forgive?

Step 2: Consider starting a "forgiveness journal," beginning with what you wrote down in step 1. Making this a daily practice, for just five or ten minutes a day, can jump-start a habit of forgiveness in your life. It will be helpful to break your journal into sections:

Phase One: In this initial phase tell your story. This can include venting about what happened, what created your anger and bitterness, and why you are having a hard time forgiving.

Phase Two: After you've expressed the hurt, it is important not to stay there and let it simmer even more. Instead, try to start turning your story into a positive learning experience. So on the next few pages don't focus on *who* hurt you; rather, focus on the hurt feeling itself and how it has affected you. How has the hurt held you back? How have you suffered from holding on to the hurt? How has it affected your past and present relationships? Did it lead you to be self-protective and isolated?

Phase Three: In this phase of the forgiveness process build on your understanding of your own reactions to the hurt, with a focus on healing and what you need to move past the hurt. Answer these questions in your journal: What lessons did you learn? How can you use the insights you gained to make you a wiser and more compassionate person? How can you get stronger by overcoming what made you weak? Look for solutions to overcome the problems. Allow your hurts to deepen you instead of weaken you.

Step 3: To help you process your thoughts, here's a quick quiz to serve as a self-check to help you on the journey of forgiveness.

Forgiveness is not a "once and done" process—keep revisiting these steps and take this quiz periodically, noticing whether you make some improvements over time.

How Forgiving Are You?

For the following 10 questions, rate each item from 1 to 10 in your journal to find your "forgiveness IQ."

1	2	3	4	5	6	7	8	9	10

Strongly Disagree   **Strongly Agree**

_____ I refuse to forgive others who are not sorry for what they have done.

_____ Forgiving someone who has wronged me is letting them "off the hook."

_____ My inability to forgive leaves me controlled too much by my past.

_____ If I forgive, it will be condoning the bad behavior.

_____ I have a hard time trusting others because of those who have hurt me.

_____ If I forgive, it makes the person or people not accountable for their actions.

_____ I have little control over being able to forgive if it does not come naturally.

_____ My hurt isolates me rather than brings me closer to others.

_____ I need to protect myself from being hurt again, and it is hard to open up.

_____ I have a hard time forgiving both myself and others for all my past mistakes, cluelessness, and choices.

_____ **Total**

How did you do? The lower the score, the better your forgiveness IQ.

15 or lower: You are a forgiveness expert! Congratulations!

16–29: You have given yourself the gift of forgiveness and can stay positive.

30–49: You have some work to do on becoming less negative and stuck in past resentments.

50–69: Being unable to forgive has handicapped you in your present life.

70–84: The past has too much power over your present and has robbed you of the growth you need to move forward in a positive direction. Consider seeking professional help.

85–100: Danger zone! Mental health and even physical health is threatened by your emotional crippling. Consider seeking psychological help.

45: Develop "Bigger-Than-Yourself" Goals

"The more you lose yourself in something bigger than yourself, the more energy you will have."

—Norman Vincent Peale

One of the surest ways to feel better about yourself is to help others. Perhaps that is why volunteerism often helps the person volunteering as much as the person who is helped. In fact, the link between happiness and helping others is well documented. Many people have found that the rewards reaped from the causes and activities they devote themselves to far outweigh the effort given to them. Volunteerism and giving of ourselves help us stay connected to others and provide us with a sense of serving a higher purpose outside of ourselves. That is why I have a favorite motto: "Want to feel better? Help someone else!"

Kelly McGonigal's research (2016) shows that when we are generous with our resources of time, money, caring, and compassion, we end up feeling better than those with a self-focused mind-set. So what matters isn't your IQ or your skill level in any particular area, but rather, how much you pursue goals for a common good. McGonigal believes that having "bigger-than-yourself" goals ends up making you more productive and successful in your personal goals as well.

How about you? Have you noticed a connection in your life between having goals that are beyond yourself and your ability to feel good about yourself? Have you found that giving of yourself boosts your self-confidence?

GIVE IT A TRY

Setting goals that are larger than you can improve your sense of self-confidence and self-esteem.

Step 1: Ask yourself if some of your goals include bigger-than-yourself goals, which help you find meaning and purpose in feeling engaged and connected to others. These are some questions to answer in your journal to help you arrive at goals that will increase your sense of connectedness and meaning:

- *How can I make a positive impact on my life and on those around me?*

- *What inspires me?*

- *What is or can be my personal mission to give meaning to my life and to those around me?*

- *Instead of feeling in competition with others, how can I facilitate cooperation?*

- *What would I like to contribute to the world?*

- *What changes would I like to create in my life and in the lives of others?*

- *How would a shift from a self-focused goal to a bigger-than-self goal help me?*

Step 2: After brainstorming and journaling your responses to the above questions, decide on at least one positive action you can take this week to commit to a bigger-than-yourself goal. What behavioral changes can you make? What can you get involved with to help you feel connected to a greater good? Do you need to change your attitude about something you already do, to incorporate a bigger-than-yourself aspect into a self-focused goal?

Step 3: Now think long range of how you can be in a supportive network to pursue bigger-than-yourself goals. Would that entail joining a spiritual or religious group, church or synagogue? Joining a political or social organization? Doing community service that can provide a forum for engagement and connection with others? The choices we make to pursue a meaningful life within a context of involvement can help us feel connected, supported, and loved.

Whenever you feel alone and distant from others, think of how you can involve yourself in bigger-than-yourself goals that will provide you with a sense of involvement, connection, and meaning.

Embrace Your Life

LOVING YOURSELF AND LOVING YOUR LIFE

When much of sixty-seven-year-old Thomas Edison's inventions went up in smoke when his workspace was destroyed in a catastrophic fire, instead of triggering extreme stress and despair in him, Edison calmly asked his son to go get his mother so she could watch, as "she will never see anything like this as long as she lives." The next day he said, "There is a great value in disaster. All our mistakes have burned up. Thank God we can start anew."

A modern-day example of this attitude is that of the late Steve Jobs. In his 2005 Stanford commencement speech Jobs shared that being kicked out of Apple, the company he founded, was both humiliating and a chance to start anew. What would have been to most of us a huge public failure and embarrassment became an impetus to bounce back better than ever. "I didn't see it then, but it turned out that getting fired from Apple was the best thing that could have ever happened to me," he said. "The heaviness of being successful was replaced by the lightness of being a beginner again, less sure about everything. It freed me to enter one of the most creative periods of my life."

This ability to accept a major setback or even a tragic, life-changing disaster is an illustration of *positive psychology*, one of the newest and most popular fields of study in psychology currently, which focuses on how we can be happier and increase our sense of well-being. In their reactions to what many of us would surely deem gut-wrenching and devastating challenges, people like Edison and Jobs have the resiliency, equanimity, and optimism to see the growth potential in traumatic events. Instead of focusing on what has been lost, they focus on what is left, to move forward and create anew.

The founder of positive psychology, Martin Seligman (2004), shifted from the study of "mental illness" to "mental wellness," addressing how individuals and communities can increase their emotional health, well-being, and resiliency. Rather than focusing on cognitive distortions, mental disturbances, and dysfunction, positive psychology teaches us what makes people thrive and grow personally, socially, and spiritually. The focus of positive psychology is solutions, not problems.

In this chapter we will delve into some important concepts of positive psychology to find out how we can learn to be emotionally well even when the world lets us down. We will explore the exciting new branch of positive psychology called *mind-set science*, which demonstrates the power of our mind in shaping our emotions, our actions, and even our physical health.

Are you ready to embrace your life, love yourself, and find the happiness you deserve?

46: Be Positive and Optimistic

"Whether you think you can, or you think you can't—
you're right."

—Henry Ford

Do you have an optimistic or a pessimistic way of thinking? Martin Seligman (2006) uses the term *negative explanatory style* to refer to the tendency to think in pessimistic ways, whereas a *positive explanatory style* applies to those who are more optimistic and positive in their thinking. Seligman explains that a negative explanatory style leads to "learned helplessness" and depression. He points out that someone with a pessimistic explanatory style interprets setbacks as permanent instead of temporary, global instead of specific, and due to fundamental personal flaws that are unchangeable.

For example, a person with a negative explanatory style who unsuccessfully tries to get date for a party will explain the perceived failure as global ("Things never work out for me"), permanent ("I'll never meet anyone"), and self-blaming ("I am unlikable"). Conversely, a person with a positive explanatory style, someone who has learned to be optimistic and resilient, will interpret being unable to get a date as something that is changeable with time, circumstance, and effort, and they will not see the lack of success as proof of being fundamentally unlovable or a failure.

How about you? Do you have a negative explanatory style? If so, isn't it time to change?

GIVE IT A TRY

Even if it seems like it is second nature to look at your life through the filter of a negative explanatory style, never lose sight of the fact that you can change your filter by learning how to think in more optimistic ways. Here are some concrete steps to help you do that:

Step 1: Identify a handful of situations that have been difficult for you and record them in your journal. For example, *I went to a singles mixer and didn't meet anyone.*

Step 2: Divide a blank page into two columns, to create a table like the one on the next page, with the same column headings. Under the first column write out your unhealthy interpretation of a situation, then pair it on the right with a more optimistic and realistic interpretation.

Notice in the second column how much kinder the self-statements are, how much more workable the situation becomes just by interpreting what happens in a less global, pessimistic, and self-critical way. Here are some examples to get you started:

Negative Explanatory Style	Positive Explanatory Style
Nobody likes me—I'm just unlikable.	*It's a tough forum for me to meet people, and there was no one I "clicked" with.*
I'll never meet anyone and will spend my life alone.	*I just haven't found the right person yet. But I can't predict the future and I see no reason why I couldn't meet someone if I want to.*
Things just don't work out for me.	*I have been successful in school and in my career. I will never stop trying.*

Step 3: Recall the proverbial example of a cup being either "half empty" or "half full." Draw a glass with a line intersecting it in the middle. In the bottom half write some of your negative explanations, and in the top half write your more positive alternative explanations. Using this visualization often will help you redirect your thinking in more optimistic ways. Consider using the simple diagram of a half-empty/half-full cup to regularly write out your negative thoughts and turn them into more positive ones.

Learning simple strategies to turn your negative interpretations into healthier versions will change your outlook, change your life, and help you achieve a sense of unshakable self-esteem.

47: Have an Attitude of Gratitude

"When a person doesn't have gratitude, something is missing in his or her humanity."

—Elie Wiesel

Gratefulness is perhaps one of the most important ingredients to an optimistic and resilient life. People who are grateful tend to be forgiving, loving, and hopeful. But when things go wrong, do you ever wonder what you really have to be grateful for?

It certainly is easier to be grateful when things are going well in your life and you feel like you are on a winning team. It is much harder to be grateful when life throws you curveballs. If you find yourself losing more than you are winning and can't seem to get over past regrets, disappointments, and life's injustices, gratefulness is a hard nut to crack. Experiencing loss, frustration, and even trauma, especially if we feel blindsided, can make it hard to "feel the love." Yet, no matter what happens to us, if we "dig deep," we can often find that there is really plenty to be thankful for in our lives.

These are some characteristics of grateful people:

- They don't expect to have a rainbow without the rain.

- They change what they can but accept what they cannot change, without railing against life's injustices.

- They don't look for what is missing in their lives—they focus on the gifts they are given.

- They do not have preconditions to their happiness. Instead of thinking they'll be happy *when*, they look at what they have *now*.

- They spend little time comparing themselves to others; being bitter, jealous, or resentful.

- They define themselves by their dreams and determination, not their disappointments.

How about you? Are you grateful, or do you focus on the "holes" in your life instead of the "whole"?

GIVE IT A TRY

If you make gratitude a priority in your life, your focus will shift from negativity to positivity. There are many ways to incorporate gratitude in your everyday life.

Step 1: Start the day with an expression of gratitude. What ritual can you add to your life to begin each day with a reminder to be thankful? Jot down some ideas, pick one to commit to each morning, and consider ending your day with this gratitude ritual as well. For example, place a photo of loved ones by your bed, and start and end each day with thanks that they are in your life.

Step 2: Keep a "gratitude journal," writing down at least three things you are grateful for every day. Do not use the same items over again—the idea is to think of at least three new things every day. Tough to do? That's the point! Keep looking for what makes you grateful instead of bitter. Keeping thoughts of gratitude at the forefront of your mind will help you feel better about yourself and your life.

Step 3: Like the "should jar" suggested in tip #10, consider having a "gratitude jar," in which you put slips of paper containing reasons you are grateful. Continually add to your jar, filling it with words or drawings on note cards that reflect your thankfulness. Keeping this jar in a prominent place will remind you of the importance of a grateful mind-set.

Step 4: Spread the positivity around! Every day make an effort to tell at least one person something you are grateful for about them.

At every opportunity look for ways to be grateful, express gratitude, and use gratefulness practices to feel good about yourself and to feel great about your life!

48: Stress for Success

"The best way to manage stress isn't to reduce or avoid it, but rather to rethink and even embrace it."

—Kelly McGonigal

What first comes to mind when I ask you to fill in the blank: "Stress is _____"? If you are like most people, your answers will likely show a negative view of stress, with responses such as "difficult," "harmful," "overwhelming," "too much to do and too little time," "debilitating." Only a small percentage of the time do I hear positive descriptions of stress, such as "motivating," "exciting," "necessary for growth." The truth is that stress has both positive and negative aspects.

After getting a string of mostly unfavorable reviews on stress from either my clients or in my wellness trainings, I point out that even having the notion that stress is bad for you is a problem in itself. In fact, research has shown that if we even *think* stress is bad for us, we tend to be less stress-resilient, more depressed, more anxious, and less likely to find meaning and challenge in our lives. The truth is that stress is not inherently "good" or "bad"—it just *is*. Stress is just part of life, and the more we try to avoid it, the more we will be disturbed by it.

This concept is not just wishful thinking—it is supported by numerous research studies that show that stress can be helpful and even invigorating. Stress can energize us and help us feel involved and engaged.

Are you ready to change your relationship to stress, making it meaningful in your life? Instead of avoiding stress, how about embracing it?

GIVE IT A TRY

Embracing stress rather than avoiding it might seem counterintuitive, but developing some habits that will allow you to positively view stress will help you on your journey to growth and self-discovery.

Step 1: Visualize your stress as a string of an instrument, such as a guitar. If you tighten the string too much, it will snap. If you do not tighten it enough, the sound will drone. This metaphor represents the fine balance of stress we need to have in our lives. Too much stress can burn us out, but too little stress and involvement with the outside world will leave us feeling isolated, alienated, disengaged, and depressed.

Step 2: Write a list of ten to twenty things in your life that you find stressful, including both negative and positive stressors. They can be relatively minor, such as working with a difficult client (negative stressor) or watching your child play in the big game (positive stressor), or they can be pretty major, like coping with an illness or dealing with trauma (negative) or planning a vacation, receiving a promotion, or getting married (positive).

Step 3: Once you compose your list, put a plus sign next to each item you consider a positive stressor and a minus sign by each you consider a negative stressor. For those marked with a minus sign think of ways to turn them into positives. For example, *Having to work with a demanding client is teaching me patience and provides an opportunity to work on my assertiveness skills.*

Step 4: Instead of avoiding dealing with your stress, what can you do to help heal from it? Examples could be opening up to others and disclosing more, reaching out to others for help and support rather than "trying to go it alone," and sharing thoughts and feelings rather than keeping them bottled in.

It is not stressors themselves that make or break us; rather, it is our thoughts about those life stressors that determine if we are debilitated by them or motivated by them. So instead of trying to avoid stress, how about embracing it?

49: Shift Your Mind-Set, Change Your Life

"It's not always the people who start out the smartest who end up the smartest."

—Carol Dweck

Our mind-set affects not only our mental health, but our physical health as well. Money, status, and material success offer us less of an edge than most people think when it comes to our level of life happiness and life satisfaction. There is actually a term for the new field of positive psychology that studies happiness and well-being in this way—it's known as "mind-set science."

According to mind-set psychologist Carol Dweck (2007), the brightest people are not necessarily the happiest or even the most successful. Rather, the main determinant of happiness and life satisfaction is having a "growth mind-set" over a "fixed mind-set" in reaction to life's setbacks, including failures. Here are some ways the two outlooks differ:

Growth Mind-Set	Fixed Mind-Set
Work and effort are most important	Natural intelligence and past achievements are most important
Believes abilities can be altered	Believes abilities are fixed and unchangeable
Determination can pay off	Determination matters less than innate ability
Appreciates the importance of persistence and effort	Thinks effort is less important than natural skill
Goal is to grow	Goal is to appear smart and successful
Focus is on the process of learning	Focus is on successful outcomes
Tends to be open-minded	Tends to be more defensive and closed-minded
Tends to be flexible and open to feedback	Tends to be self-protective
Perseveres after failure	Defeated by failure

Do you tend to have a growth mind-set, or are you held back by a fixed mind-set? If your mind-set tends to be more fixed, are you ready to shift it? Isn't it about time?

GIVE IT A TRY

Taking steps to change a fixed mind-set to a more flexible, positive mind-set will be key to improving your self-esteem and self-confidence.

Step 1: Look at the different descriptions of the two types of mind-sets on the previous page. Which alternative better matches your way of thinking?

Step 2: For each characteristic of a fixed mind-set that you identify with, write a sentence or two to transform it into a growth mind-set characteristic.

Step 3: For a hands-on activity to remind you of the importance of a growth mind-set, draw something that has meaning for you. If you are like most people, your initial reaction will be to think, *I can't draw* or *I'm not good at drawing*. You might even question what is the *right* thing to draw!

These thoughts reflect a fixed mind-set—defining yourself by your preconceptions about yourself or your concern over what you are "supposed to do" or "how good" you are at something. Instead, with a growth mind-set mentality, focus on enjoying the act of drawing as a vehicle of self-expression, without concern for whether or not you are "good" at it. Just enjoy the process of expressing yourself artistically without judgment.

How does it feel to change your negative self-talk to a growth mind-set? Can you appreciate what a difference it will make in your life to make your focus on your growth rather than on things you cannot change? Can you see how choosing a growth mind-set will set you free from self-imposed road-blocks, allowing you to move forward with more optimism and freedom to grow?

50: Live an Emotionally Resilient Life

"To love oneself is the beginning of a lifelong romance."

—Oscar Wilde

We all know in theory how to eat well, and we all also know about the importance of exercise to increase our chances of living longer and healthier. Even if it is hard to stick to a plan, we know in general what is good for us.

Pinpointing the guidelines for emotional wellness, however, is not as obvious for most of us. The softer skills of emotional wellness also need practice and attention, and just like we can change our diet and exercise habits with attention, we have the power to change our level of mental and emotional fitness.

The quiz below revisits the ten areas we touched on in this book that will lead to loving yourself, to setting a foundation of emotional wellness and unshakable self-esteem. Use this as a tool to measure how you fare now in these ten areas, and as you return to certain chapters or areas of the book where you feel you need extra work, this quiz will help you assess if you are making some improvement.

Emotional wellness and self-esteem go hand in hand. The more you like yourself, the more emotionally well you are. Regardless of where you started, you can learn skills to improve your mental fitness and boost your self-esteem so you can live the awesome life that awaits you!

GIVE IT A TRY

Take the following quiz to get a snapshot of your emotional fitness as you work toward securing a strong foundation of self-love and unshakable self-esteem.

Emotional Wellness Quiz

In your journal, rate your level of agreement with each statement listed (making sure to be honest and open with yourself).

7—Strongly agree

6—Mostly agree

5—Slightly agree

4—Neither agree nor disagree

3—Slightly disagree

2—Mostly disagree

1—Strongly disagree

_____ My self-esteem is unconditional, and I am accepting and loving of myself.

_____ I can laugh at life's imperfections, as well as my own, and see the humor in things.

_____ I have healthy thinking habits and tend to look at things objectively and rationally.

_____ I do not hold on to regrets, and disappointments and regrets motivate me, not debilitate me.

_____ I am self-compassionate and loving to myself, and I refuse to beat myself up with self-criticism.

_____ I live in the present mindfully rather than being torn between ruminations of the past and anxieties of the future.

_____ My self-care is a priority, and I have good self-care habits.

_____ I tend to be assertive, expressing my thoughts and feelings while respecting the rights of others.

_____ I have a good support system and have people to confide in.

_____ I am motivated by my stress and find meaning and gratefulness in life's challenges and struggles.

_____ **Total**

Emotional Wellness Score Range

62–70: Awesome level of emotional wellness—you rock!

54–61: High level of emotional wellness

46–53: Moderate level of emotional wellness

38–45: Emotional wellness needs some boosting

30–37: Emotional wellness is problematic

22–29: Emotional wellness is low and needs attention and help to improve mood and coping

Below 22: Danger zone—professional help to improve your emotional wellness is highly indicated!

Closing Thoughts

The intent of this book has been to help you thrive in the most important relationship you will ever have: your relationship with yourself. If your relationship with yourself is not good, your relationships with others and your life in general will also suffer. Self-doubt and low self-esteem will rob you of the happy and fulfilling life you deserve and will handicap your relationships in all areas of your life.

The more you love yourself, the more you will trust others and be able to develop strong connections that are healthy and mature rather than needy, demanding, dependent, enabling, or possessive. Whether you are someone's child, parent, spouse, partner, coworker, or friend, the healthier your self-view, the more you will be able to balance giving to yourself with giving to those close to you.

I hope that you have found some of the tips and activities in this book helpful in allowing you to truly embrace your greatness. Remember that you are a miracle. The chances of you being precisely *you*, among all of the trillions of genetic combinations that could have occurred, is not something to take for granted. Life is precious and special, and so are you. Don't let anyone—including yourself—ever lose sight of that fundamental truth.

If you started this journey not sure if you were "good enough," or just feeling too fundamentally flawed to ever truly accept yourself, I hope this book has given you the information and support you need to see yourself as a beautiful human being worthy of self-love and love from others. No matter what happened in the past, what choices you made that you now regret; no matter if your personal defeats far outnumber your personal triumphs, your greatness still remains the same and deserves to be recognized and embraced.

After you finish this book, it will be helpful to revisit certain parts that cover topics you need to work on most. Revisiting the concepts and doing the exercises over and over again will help you practice new skills and master the ability to eliminate your self-doubt, boost your self-esteem, and increase your resiliency. Undoing years of unhealthy habits of thinking and behaving takes a lot of work and practice, so be patient with your progress and just focus on moving forward, with increased wisdom and courage.

Whether you succeed or you fall short, whether you win or lose, whether you stand tall or feel small, as long as you keep striving for goodness as you grow, heal, and evolve, you already are achieving greatness. Sometimes you will reach far beyond your grasp, but remember that even when things don't turn out great, *you* still can!

Greatness is part of the journey, it's not found only in the destination. As your life unfolds, I wish you a lifelong journey of hope, commitment, positivity, growth, and healing so you can truly love yourself to love your life. You deserve it!

References

Achor, S. 2010. *The Happiness Advantage: The Seven Principles of Positive Psychology That Fuel Success and Performance at Work.* New York: Random House.

Beck, A. 1967. *The Diagnosis and Management of Depression.* Philadelphia: University of Pennsylvania Press.

Beck, A. 1972. *Depression: Causes and Treatment.* Philadelphia: University of Pennsylvania Press.

Beck, A. 1976. *Cognitive Therapy and the Emotional Disorders.* New York: International University Press.

Bourne, E. 2010. *The Anxiety and Phobia Workbook.* Oakland, CA: New Harbinger Publications.

Brown, B. 2010. *The Gifts of Imperfection: Let Go of Who You Think You're Supposed to Be and Embrace Who You Are.* Center City, MN: Hazelden.

Burns, D. D. 1980. "The Perfectionist's Script for Self-Defeat." *Psychology Today* (November): 34–52.

Burns, D. D. 1989. *The Feeling Good Handbook.* New York: William Morrow.

Burns, D. D. 1999. *Ten Days to Self-Esteem.* New York: William Morrow.

Burns, D. D. 2008. *Feeling Good: The New Mood Therapy*. New York: Harper.

Doran, G. T. 1981. "There's a S.M.A.R.T. Way to Write Management's Goals and Objectives." *Management Review* 70 (11): 35–36.

Dweck, C. 2007. *Mindset: The New Psychology of Success*. New York: Ballantine Books.

Ellis, A. 1957. "Rational Psychotherapy and Individual Psychology." *Journal of Individual Psychology* 13: 38–44.

Gordon, T. 1977. *Leader Effectiveness Training: L.E.T.* New York: G. P. Putnam's Sons.

Guise, S. 2013. *Mini Habits: Smaller Habits, Bigger Results*. CreateSpace Independent Publishing Platform.

Hayes, S. 2005. *Get Out of Your Mind and Into Your Life: The New Acceptance and Commitment Therapy*. Oakland, CA: New Harbinger Publications.

Kabat-Zinn, J. 2005. *Coming to Our Senses: Healing the World and Ourselves Through Mindfulness*. New York: Hyperion.

Kübler-Ross, E. 1969. *On Death and Dying*. New York: Simon & Schuster.

Kushner, H. 1997. *How Good Do We Have to Be? A New Understanding of Guilt and Forgiveness*. New York: Back Bay Books.

McGonigal, K. 2016. *The Upside of Stress: Why Stress Is Good for You, and How to Get Good at It*. New York: Avery.

Neff, K. 2011. *Self-Compassion: The Proven Power of Being Kind to Yourself*. New York: HarperCollins.

Roese, N. 2005. *If Only: How to Turn Regret into Opportunity*. New York: Random House.

Rogers, C. 1956. *Client-Centered Therapy*. 3rd ed. Boston: Houghton-Mifflin.

Schaub, L. 2013. *The Self-Esteem Workbook for Teens: Activities to Help You Build Confidence and Achieve Your Goals*. Oakland, CA: Instant Help Publications.

Schiraldi, G. 2001. *The Self-Esteem Workbook*. Oakland, CA: New Harbinger Publications.

Seligman, M. 2004. *Authentic Happiness: Using the New Positive Psychology to Realize Your Potential for Lasting Fulfillment*. New York: Atria Books.

Seligman, M. 2006. *Learned Optimism: How to Change Your Mind and Your Life*. New York: Vintage Books.

Taylor, S., et al. 2000. "Biobehavioral Responses to Stress in Females: Tend-and-Befriend, Not Fight-or-Flight." *Psychological Review* 107 (3): 411–429.

Taylor, S. 2002. *The Tending Instinct: Women, Men, and the Biology of Our Relationships*. New York: Holt.

Tedeschi, R. G., and L. G. Calhoun. 2004. "Posttraumatic Growth: Conceptual Foundations and Empirical Evidence." *Psychological Inquiry* 15 (1): 1–18.

Judith Belmont, MS, LPC, has been a psychotherapist, motivational speaker, workplace wellness consultant, and mental health coach. Her message of positivity, healthy communication, stress resilience, and self-empowerment has reached thousands nationwide through her books, consulting, and interactive presentations.

She is author of seven mental health and wellness books that offer therapists and their clients, as well as self-help readers, practical solutions to deal with common problems such as low self-esteem, depression, anxiety, and relationship issues. In her books, she offers practical skill-building resources using experiential activities, visualizations, handouts, and worksheets.

Belmont is founder of Belmont Wellness (www.belmontwell ness.com) where she offers a variety of mental health and wellness presentations, as well as personal and professional coaching. Her mission to share important life skills and promote self-empowerment and positivity is followed by a wide audience due to her active social media presence on various sites such as Facebook and Pinterest.

Register your **new harbinger** titles for additional benefits!

When you register your **new harbinger** title—purchased in any format, from any source—you get access to benefits like the following:

- Downloadable accessories like printable worksheets and extra content

- Instructional videos and audio files

- Information about updates, corrections, and new editions

Not every title has accessories, but we're adding new material all the time.

Access free accessories in 3 easy steps:

1. Sign in at NewHarbinger.com (or **register** to create an account).

2. Click on **register a book**. Search for your title and click the **register** button when it appears.

3. Click on the **book cover or title** to go to its details page. Click on **accessories** to view and access files.

That's all there is to it!

If you need help, visit:

NewHarbinger.com/accessories

new harbinger
CELEBRATING
40 YEARS